The economics of militarism

Militarism, State and Society

Series editor: Dan Smith

Pluto's series on militarism, state and society provides
political analysis as well as new information and argument
relating to current political controversies in the field of
nuclear weapons, military policy and disarmament. It aims
to present radical analyses and critiques of the existing
orthodoxies in readable and accessible form.

Dan Smith and Ron Smith

The economics
of militarism

Pluto  Press

First published in 1983 by
Pluto Press Limited,
The Works, 105a Torriano Avenue,
London NW5 2RX

Copyright © Dan Smith and Ron Smith, 1983

Cover designed by Clive Challis A.Gr.R.
Cover photomontage by Peter Kennard

Photoset by Photobooks (Bristol) Ltd.
Printed in Great Britain by St Edmundsbury Press, Suffolk

British Library Cataloguing in Publication Data
Smith, Dan
    The economics of militarism.
    1. Militarism—Economic aspects
    I. Title   II. Smith, Ron
    355'.0213   U21.2

    ISBN 0-86104-370-7

Contents

Acknowledgements / 7
Introduction / 9

1. **Military expenditure** / 14
   Military numbers / 15
   World military spending / 22
   British military spending / 27

2. **The drive to militarism** / 40
   Strategic requirements / 41
   International militarism / 45
   Domestic militarism / 50
   Soviet militarism / 54

3. **The foundations of militarism** / 62
   The military and bureaucracy / 62
   Industry and technology / 71

4. **The economic consequences of military spending** / 83
   Immediate effects / 84
   Longer-term effects / 90
   Unemployment / 96
   Economic motivations of military spending / 99

5. **The economics of disarmament** / 102
   Industrial and economic conversion / 104
   The international environment / 113

Notes and references / 121

Acknowledgements

This book draws on research supported by various bodies to whom we are deeply grateful. Ron Smith's research was financed by a number of SSRC grants to the Department of Economics, Birkbeck College. Research into western European arms industries and policies by Dan Smith at Birkbeck was financed by the Deutsche Gesellschaft fur Friedens- und Konfliktforschung and by the Joseph Rowntree Charitable Trust. A grant from the United Nations to both of us financed work on the resource costs of armaments and the economic consequences of disarmament. In thanking them all for their support, we must emphasise that our arguments and conclusions in this book are our own and do not represent the views of these bodies.

We have other debts of gratitude to express, especially to Saadet Deger and Clare Mundy for research assistance. The Department of Economics at Birkbeck made it possible for us both to work there and have the chance to discuss the many issues of militarism in detail over an extended period and jointly produce other written material. We thank the department institutionally, and also our colleagues there individually. The impetus towards this particular work was provided partly by the interest of Pluto Press and partly by an invitation to co-teach a course on defence economics at the University of York's Department of Economics in autumn 1980. We particularly thank Douglas Dosser and Keith Hartley at York for this opportunity, and Richard Kuper at Pluto for sustaining his interest and patience through the book's long gestation.

Discussions with many people over the years have helped

us elaborate and elucidate our ideas. In particular, Ron Smith thanks Sam Aaronovitch, Jean Gardiner and Roger Moore, co-authors of *The Political Economy of British Capitalism*, and Dan Smith thanks Michael Brzoska, Peter Lock and Herbert Wulf, co-researchers in problems of western European military industry. Linda Hesselman, Mary Kaldor and Jill Lewis made valuable comments on an early draft. Naturally, all responsibility for what appears in this book rests with us.

February 1983

Introduction

In 1982 military spending worldwide was about $600,000,000,000. In the less developed countries, about 800 million people lived in absolute poverty. In advanced capitalist countries, people were plagued by recession and mass unemployment. The world was threatened by growing tensions and the risk of nuclear war.

In this book we hope to provide some insights into the causes and consequences of high military spending and what can be done about it. We take military spending as the starting point for an enquiry into the economics of militarism and in focusing on this aspect we hope to contribute to a wider understanding of the whole problem.

Our intention is to provide an introduction to the issues. We have therefore tried to make the book as compact and as accessible as possible. This has had two consequences. First, we decided not to enter into a detailed discussion of the USSR's military spending and policies. Our focus is for the most part upon the advanced capitalist countries although we do include a general discussion of questions related to the USSR in chapter 2. This is not because we think the grass is greener in the USSR, but because a proper discussion of it would require a depth of treatment which would make this a different and much longer book. Similarly, we do not offer much discussion of the poor countries. The second consequence of opting for brevity is that we have touched on a number of questions without going into much detail. We have sought often to illustrate our arguments with examples rather than prove them. Readers who wish to follow up on our arguments will find some of them more fully discussed in our previous works (especially *The Political Economy of British Capitalism, The Defence of the Realm in the 1980s* and our joint essay in *Protest and Survive*), or in other works cited in the Notes. *The War Atlas* provides a graphic representation of many of the issues we discuss.[1]

Chapter 1 discusses the figures which have to be used to understand military spending, and the problems within those figures. It also looks at the British military budget as a specific case study. The initial focus is on the economics of militarism, but the problem is clearly not purely economic. Military spending is rooted in complex social and political processes. Chapter 2 discusses the requirement for military spending, and stresses the self-interested rationality of that requirement given the goals, positions and environment of the major political actors. Chapter 3 emphasises the irrational ways in which that requirement is met by the military and industrial institutions which form the social foundation of military spending. Chapter 4 discusses the economic consequences of military spending. Unlike many radical writers, we do not believe that military spending is economically functional for advanced capitalism. Rather, we see it as a political requirement which is an economic burden. Finally, chapter 5 looks at the economic components of a disarmament programme, but again argues that the decisive issues are ultimately political.

Two issues are worth commenting on at this stage. They are the definition of 'militarism' and the meaning of 'rationality'.

The term 'militarism' is widely used to refer to a number of different things – high military spending, bellicose foreign policies and a propensity to fight wars, large arms industries, the promotion of military values in society, military dictatorship and government by martial law. These are often seen as if they are the heads of a Hydra-type beast. Militarism is then seen as a uniform, underlying and causative process which produces these various phenomena. The result of this approach is an effort to characterise the quintessence of militarism, an effort which has so far been fruitless as far as we can see.[2]

We believe this effort has been fruitless because there is no such single process and no necessary relationship between the various phenomena. Some countries have relatively high military spending but not much arms industry. Others have military dictatorships which show little propensity to war. Many of the states which have most often resorted to war, like Britain, have never been run by the military.

For us, the term 'militarism' is descriptive rather than analytic. It denotes the various things we have listed, in which the common keynote is the maintenance of permanent armed forces. It names the effects of various causes – not the cause of various effects. To the extent that the causes of militarism are linked, the connections must be sought in the social and economic foundations of the states which maintain permanent armed forces and the international system within which they operate.

The comment about the meaning of rationality is really a comment about the style of our analysis and discussion. Edward Thompson has sounded an important warning note about rational analyses of militarism:

> [T]o structure an analysis in a consecutive rational manner may be, at the same time, to impose a consequential rationality upon the object of analysis. What if the object is *ir*rational? What if events are being willed by no single causative historical logic . . . a logic which then may be analysed in terms of origins, intentions or goals, contradictions or conjunctures – but are simply the product of a messy inertia?[3]

Indeed, if the outcome of current events is to be a nuclear holocaust, we could be forgiven for declaring the whole business insane and leaving it there.

But we think the important point in Thompson's warning is the need to distinguish between the rational and the irrational. This, however, depends on asking, rational for whom? In chapter 2 we argue that there is a requirement, based on the self-interested political rationality of the rulers, for high military spending in the advanced capitalist countries and the USSR. The rationality 'belongs' to the leaders of these states. It does not mean these policies are desirable or even tolerable – merely that, from a certain standpoint, they are rational, the actions are consistent with their goals. The argument becomes more complicated. If each state follows courses which are individually rational, there could still be an irrational outcome such as a global nuclear war. Mathematical Game Theory has produced many studies of the way in which a collision between two rational actions can produce a result neither party desired.[4] So the fact that behaviour is rational does not mean it is safe – not even for those for whom it is rational. Yet further complications enter when we consider that different actors within the whole process of military spending have different standpoints, and therefore different criteria by which to assess what is rational. States' strategic requirements for military spending are often met in profoundly irrational and self-defeating ways, yet for those whose task is to meet the requirements, the processes and results appear quite rational. What seems rational to one may seem irrational to another because a different timespan is being used in assessing what is and is not rational. In the long term, it is as irrational for arms manufacturers as it is for the rest of us, to feed an uncontrolled nuclear arms race; in the short term, it is highly rational for them since it provides profits.

The result of all this is that the book involves numerous switches of focus and language. We want to show as much as possible the roots of the processes involved in military spending. Our view is that these processes appear to those who manage them to be rational. But when we describe an action or policy as rational, that does not mean we necessarily agree with it, nor that it is rational for all those involved in managing military spending. As we shift in analysis from one level of policy to another, so we shift the level of criticism and language depending on whether the preconceptions we are using are those of states, militaries, bureaucracies, corporations or our own.

Finally, then, we ought to indicate at the outset of the book that our own preconceptions are that it is important to take the long-term view, and that within that perspective those who have an interest in human survival, political freedom and economic prosperity must inevitably favour disarmament. If they think rationally, of course.

1. Military expenditure

This book sets out to explain military expenditure. But military statistics, like all other statistics, must be treated with care. Figures for military expenditure do not simply provide information; they also serve to disinform the general public, to create a cult of the expert in which the subject becomes so complex that only a few responsible authorities have the right or ability to analyse them, and use them as tools of crude propaganda to support a particular government view and policy.

However, the statistics should not simply be dismissed out of hand. Better to understand them, the ways in which they are produced, the social relations they reflect and the theories which underlie them. It is then possible to use them to understand the military world and even to counter the ideological role they are made to play.

The first step is to recognise that there are no simple, objective facts in this field. Military statistics, whether they concern expenditure or force levels, are heavily laden with theory; they are *constructed*, not given. It is true that particular sets of figures are often interpreted in selective and slanted ways, and that there are considerable incentives for doing this – most obviously, in order to gain support for high military spending or new weapon systems. But it would be a mistake to think that somewhere, deep in the innards of military establishments, one could find 'true' and 'uncontaminated' facts. What are presented to us as 'facts' are the results of processes of estimation in which great uncertainties are involved. Military establishments themselves are subject to these uncertainties. For instance, in 1978, the senior civilian official and the senior military officer in the US Pentagon held different opinions on the number of Soviet divisions present in eastern Europe.

The second step is to be clear about what is being measured. In diagrammatic form, Figure 1.1 outlines four different concepts, the way each is measured and the intervening variables which link them. These four concepts are commonly conflated, so that the threat to security is measured by an adversary's capability, which is measured by the force levels, which in turn are measured by expenditure. But high expenditure may not buy large forces since the money can be spent inefficiently or on a small number of very expensive items. Large forces do not always produce a powerful capability since they may be unable to perform the tasks required in war having been trained for quite different tasks. Military effectiveness can only be judged in war and is in many ways inherently unknowable in advance. The American war in Vietnam is a classic case of huge expenditure and large forces failing to provide the required capability. Finally, the threat which one state poses to another's security can only be judged by reference to the former's intentions, which in turn rests on an analysis of its interests.

These preliminary points are in themselves enough to undermine much of the stock propaganda to which we are subjected. But a number of other points must be made in order to understand the statistics on military expenditure and see how very cautiously they must be treated. Accordingly, before considering the figures themselves, it is necessary to discuss the basic problems in the data.

Military numbers

What items are included in statistics for military expenditure? States differ about what should be included. For example, paramilitary forces may be included in one state's military budget but in another's police budget. Nuclear,

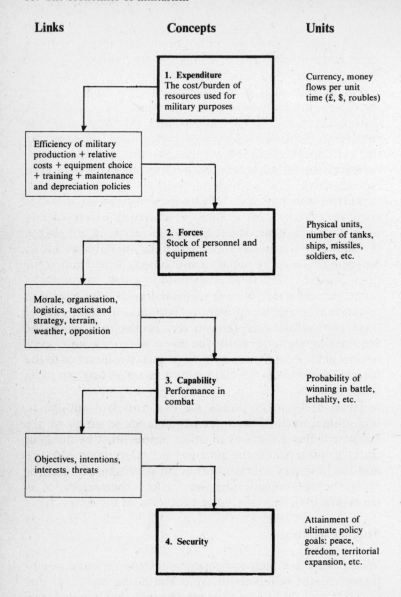

Figure 1.1 **What can you measure?**

electronic, meteorological, cartographic and space expenditures may appear in either civil or military budgets. Expenditure on health, pensions and education for military personnel and their families may or may not be included in the military budget. It is sometimes argued that the interest payable on debts incurred in fighting previous wars should be included in military budgets, but this is almost never done.

A second problem is the price basis which is used. A low-wage conscript army results in lower measured military spending than a professional army; the full cost of a conscript army is thus hidden from the measurement of military spending, even though it is a cost borne by society. The prices of many items of equipment merely represent accounting or transfer prices between different government agencies, especially when arms suppliers are owned or supported by the state. A privately owned supplier may make a loss on a particular contract and then be subsidised by the government under an industrial aid programme; the cost of that would appear in the civil budget, not in the military budget where it belongs.

There is a particular difficulty in reviewing a series of figures showing changes in real military expenditure across time. Forming such a series involves 'correcting' the figures so that the effects of inflation are cancelled out. There are many different price indexes which can be used to do this, and the choice of index influences the result. Typically, the rate of inflation for military goods and services is higher than the average rate of inflation for the country as a whole. It is, for instance, 6–10 per cent higher for military equipment for the UK according to official estimates. If the figures are deflated (i.e. the effects of inflation are removed) using a military price index, it will appear as if the real increase in military spending is lower than if an average price index is used. It can also make a difference which year is chosen as the base year in the calculations.

The third problem concerns international comparisons. To make them it is necessary to convert military expenditure from local currencies into a common currency, which is usually the US dollar. For this conversion, an exchange rate is required between the local currency and the dollar; but for some countries there may be more than one exchange rate and the final dollar figure will depend heavily on the choice of rate. Or the exchange rate may be distorted (as a result, for example, of a government policy of maintaining an artificial exchange rate) in which case it will not reflect relative prices or purchasing power in the two countries. Also, the exchange rate may fluctuate widely from year to year as a result of the esoteric workings of the international finance market, in which case changes in the dollar figure for a country's military spending may be caused by changes in the exchange rate rather than by changes in real military spending.

All these problems mean it is possible to construct more than one measure of expenditure. In general, there is no 'correct' figure – although it is often obvious when the figures are wrong. The result is that there is great scope for a creative approach to the statistics, for massaging the data to obtain the desired conclusion. These are standard problems with economic data: for example, it is well known that the official figures for unemployment simply do not include all those people without paid employment who would like it. But the problems are more severe with military data because of the constraints of secrecy and 'security', and because the political sensitivity of the numbers provides great incentives for obtaining the result which is most favourable for a particular policy.

In the UK there are three main measures of military expenditure, which differ because the definitions they use are from either the Public Expenditure White Paper, or National Income and Expenditure Accounts, or NATO. The tendency is for a government to use the higher numbers abroad to convince its allies it is contributing properly to joint defence and to convey a resolute image to its adversaries. Meanwhile, the lower figures may be used at home, to convince voters that there is no waste and no overspending on the military, or to convince them that, since military spending is relatively low, it ought to be increased.

Sources

There are two main types of data source: on the one hand, national budgets and accounts published by individual governments; on the other, a variety of estimates, either by state intelligence agencies or independent researchers, based on reports of purchases, force levels, available equipment, and so on. The three most widely used compilations of figures on military spending come from the US Arms Control and Disarmament Agency (ACDA), which makes considerable use of data produced by the Central Intelligence Agency (CIA); from the International Institute of Strategic Studies (IISS) based in London; and from the Stockholm International Peace Research Institute (SIPRI).[1]

ACDA, the IISS and SIPRI each regularly publishes detailed international comparisons of military expenditure, and the numbers differ considerably. In 1980, SIPRI published an analysis of the differences between the figures in a variety of sources from 1970 to 1975 inclusive, including figures in its own Yearbooks, and calculated standard errors for the estimates (these can be thought of as the average percentage difference between the estimates). The largest standard error was for Libya, at 85 per cent. The standard error for the USSR was 23 per cent.[2]

Soviet figures

The high standard error for figures on Soviet military spending reflects in part the irreducible technical problems of estimating how much the USSR spends. But it also reflects the political importance of the different estimates. Images of the Soviet threat are crucial for persuading public opinion in western countries to support high levels of military expenditure. Comparisons of western and Soviet military spending, purportedly showing that the USSR is 'outspending us' have been used as part of the depiction of the Soviet threat.

We could simply question the significance of these figures

by repeating that expenditure figures cannot be used to show superiority, which is a measure of relative capabilities, without specifying the intervening variables. But the political use to which these figures are put means they deserve a closer examination.

For 1979, the USSR published a military budget of 17.2 billion roubles. According to CIA estimates, the figure ought to be 58–64 billion roubles, while according to Chinese estimates it is 102 billion.[3] It may seem capricious simply to reject the official Soviet figure, but few observers in the West, whatever their politics, accept it because it barely changes from year to year, because it is not clear what is included in it, and because it seems much too low to cover the annual cost of estimated Soviet forces.

The CIA calculates Soviet military spending by first estimating the quantity of goods and services purchased – numbers of troops, tanks, missiles, ships, and so on. It then estimates what each of these would cost in the USA. Multiplying prices and quantities together produces a dollar figure which is then multiplied by an estimated rouble/dollar exchange rate to provide a total rouble figure. Finally, this is expressed as a percentage of Soviet Gross National Product (GNP) in roubles, a magnitude which must also be estimated since the USSR uses a different measure of economic output known as Net Material Product.

At each stage, the process is difficult and creates problems of bias. For example, to calculate the dollar figure it has to be assumed that Soviet troops are paid the same rates as the USA's volunteer armed forces. In fact, the bulk of Soviet military personnel are conscripts who get very low wages. One consequence of this assumption is a classic example of the problems of intelligence estimation: if US troops get a pay rise, this is fed into the CIA calculations and comes out as an apparent increase in Soviet military expenditure – the higher the US military wage, the greater the 'threat'!

There are similar problems in calculating equipment costs. American equipment tends to be more sophisticated and its price includes an element for the manufacturers' profits. Both these factors suggest the result will be to overestimate the costs of Soviet equipment, thus again artificially inflating the 'threat'.

A crucial figure in the calculations is the rouble/dollar exchange rate. The rouble is not convertible, so there is no market exchange rate – just a range of different estimates. In 1975, the CIA decided that Soviet military industry was much less efficient than had previously been thought, and it altered the exchange rate it had been using to reflect this. This did not change the dollar estimate of Soviet military spending, but it almost doubled both the rouble figure and the estimated military share of estimated GNP. The latter figure rose from 6–8 per cent to 11–13 per cent. The new figures were widely and quite erroneously taken to mean that the USSR had more military power than the CIA had previously thought. In fact, the change simply meant that Soviet military industry was now thought to be less efficient than it had previously been thought to be.

SIPRI's figures for Soviet military spending lie between the official Soviet figure and the CIA estimate. On this basis, total military spending in the USA and USSR is about the same, but because the USSR is a poorer country it must devote twice the share of annual output to achieve the same level of expenditure as the USA. This seems like a sensible compromise, and makes sense in terms of the forces and firepower each superpower is estimated to deploy. But it should be recognised that we can really have no idea what proportion of Soviet output is devoted to the military.

In the end, the attempt to compare US and Soviet military expenditures runs up hard against the problem that these two magnitudes are fundamentally and irrevocably non-comparable. In these two differently organised societies, different things have different values relative to each other. While the official Soviet budget has widespread problems of credibility, it is not beyond the bounds of possibility that it represents either all or at least the major part of actual military spending, and that the prices of goods and services are adjusted by official fiat to ensure the total budget figure remains relatively steady from year to year. Estimating Soviet military spending and the share of output it absorbs are ultimately more interesting for a study of the Soviet economy and military industry. As the basis for a comparison of US–USSR military capability, it has no intrinsic merit.

World military spending

The problem about analysing world military expenditure is that there is no very sound empirical basis on which to proceed. The estimates we must use are of varying quality: some are acceptable, produced in an estimating process as honest and rigorous as we could hope for; others are execrable. It is important to keep these qualifications in mind as we now turn to look at the figures.

In 1981, SIPRI estimated total world military spending at $600–650 billion in current prices.[4] Of this, about a quarter was spent by the USA, about a quarter by the other advanced capitalist states, and about a quarter by the USSR. Non-Soviet Warsaw Pact countries accounted for about 3 per cent of the total, and the OPEC countries for about 3 per cent.

In real terms (i.e. after correcting for inflation), total military spending has risen in recent years by about 3 per cent annually: NATO spending rose by an average of 0.9 per cent annually from 1975 to 1980; Warsaw Pact spending by an average of 1.6 per cent; and the rest of the world's military spending by an average of 4 per cent.

Table 1.1 **Shares of world military spending** (%)

	1950	1960	1970	1980
NATO	50·4	63·6	50·1	44·9
Warsaw Pact	30·4	21·8	26·5	25·7
Others	19·2	14·6	23·4	29·4

Note: In 1950 the Warsaw Pact had not actually been formed, and NATO had yet to include Greece, Turkey or West Germany; the figures shown include all countries now members of each alliance.

Source: World Armaments and Disarmament: SIPRI Yearbook 1982 (Taylor & Francis, London, 1982) and earlier issues.

Table 1.1 reflects this pattern. NATO and the Warsaw Pact countries continue to account for most of the expenditure, but their dominance of the figures was actually reduced in the 1970s. This does not reflect reduced spending by the two blocs, but rather an increasing militarisation of the rest of the world.

Table 1.2 shows figures for the military share of Gross Domestic Product (GDP) in the years 1950, 1960, 1970 and 1980 for a selection of countries. Comparing particular years can be misleading: 1950 comes just before the Korean war rearmament and, for the USA, 1960 and 1970 straddle the years of the sharpest increases in spending associated with the Vietnam war. What counts is the general trend revealed by the figures. Table 1.2 shows a general tendency for the military share of output to decline in the advanced capitalist countries, but to rise in the less developed countries.

Table 1.2 **Shares of military expenditure in GDP (%)**

	1950	1960	1970	1980
USA	5·1	9·0	8·0	5·6
France	5·5	6·5	4·2	4·1
West Germany	4·4	4·0	3·3	3·3
UK	6·6	6·5	4·8	5·1
Sweden	3·5	4·0	3·6	3·1
Japan	n.a.	1·1	0·8	1·0
Israel	4·7	5·5	23·8	[14·0]
Yugoslavia	n.a.	7·2	5·0	(4·6)*
USSR	n.a.	[12·4]	[12·0]	[9·1]*
South Africa	0·8	0·8	2·0	3·2
Saudi Arabia	n.a.	n.a.	11·8	[16·5]*
Iran	n.a.	4·3	6·6	n.a.
Brazil	2·1	2·0	1·9	0·5
India	n.a.	1·9	3·0	2·8*
Nigeria	n.a.	0·5	5·8	4·0*

Notes:

n.a.   information not available
( )   uncertain data or SIPRI estimates
[ ]   rough estimate
*   1979 figure
Source: SIPRI Yearbooks 1982 and earlier.

Figures for the years before the Second World War are not available on the same scale, but by way of comparison it can be noted that in 1938 the USA devoted 1.3 per cent of GNP to the military, the UK 6.9 per cent, and Germany about 9 per cent. Both the UK and Germany were by that time stoking up for the coming war; in the early 1930s both countries had spent around 3 per cent of GNP on the military.[5]

The countries listed in Table 1.2 do not include all the top spenders, but rather some of the strategically most important countries in different parts of the world. Two points are particularly worth noting. First, the leap in Nigeria's military spending for the war against Biafran secession became, in the 1970s, a new plateau for a permanently increased level of spending. Second, Brazil, which is all but a military dictatorship, spends a low and, atypically among less developed countries, a declining share of GDP on the military. These two examples serve to bring out the complexity and diversity of the processes we group together under the heading of 'militarism'. It will also be noted that China is missing from these tables, not because it is unimportant but because the figures in this case are more than usually unreliable – which is saying something.

Table 1.3 is a league table of the big spenders. These ten countries are, in each year shown, the world's military elite. In 1950, the top ten accounted for about 80 per cent of the world total, and about 85 per cent in 1960. As militarisation spread, the top ten's share of the world total fell to about 70 per cent in 1978. By then, two of the richest OPEC states had joined the elite, though Iran dropped out by 1980. It may also be interesting to underline that the three defeated powers of the Second World War have been in the top ten military spenders since very soon after the end of that war.

In the case of Japan, although it has tended to spend a very small proportion of its output on the military, not more than 1 per cent, a small proportion of its large output puts it in the top ten spenders.

Table 1.4 shows a variety of military comparisons between the four leading powers in NATO (although French forces are

Table 1.3 **Top ten military spenders**

1950	1960	1970	1980
USA	USA	USA	USA
USSR	USSR	USSR	USSR
UK	UK	West Germany	West Germany
France	France	France	France
West Germany	West Germany	UK	UK
Japan	Canada	Japan	Saudi Arabia
Italy	Italy	Italy	Japan
Netherlands	Japan	Netherlands	Italy
Canada	Netherlands	Canada	Netherlands
Sweden	Sweden	Australia	Canada

Source: SIPRI *Yearbook 1982* and earlier years.

Table 1.4 NATO's **big spenders, 1980**

	UK	France	USA	West Germany
Total military spending ($ bn)	24·4	20·2	142·7	25·1
Military spending ($) *per capita*	437	374	644	410
Military spending as % of GNP (1979)	4·9	3·9	5·2	3·3
Military spending as % of total government spending (1979)	10·3	17·5	21·5	22·3
People in the armed forces ('000)	329·2	494·7	2,050	495
Military spending per member of the armed forces ($'000)	74·1	40·8	69·6	50·7

Source: *The Military Balance 1980–1981* (International Institute of Strategic Studies, 1980).

not under NATO command). The basic measure, of course, is military spending itself, but other comparisons are also interesting. The comparative intensity of the military effort can be gauged both by *per capita* spending – the amount spent per head of the population – and by looking at the military burden – the proportion of national income devoted to military purposes. Comparing the proportion of government spending consumed by the military indicates how much of each state's economic activity is military-related, while comparing the level of spending per member of the armed forces may reveal different decisions about how to deploy and equip the forces.

France, the UK and West Germany spend about the same as each other on the military, while the USA spends around seven times as much (a gap which will increase if the Reagan administration's plans on military expenditure are carried through). *Per capita*, France spends slightly less than either the UK or West Germany, while the USA spends a great deal more. As a proportion of GNP, the UK and USA spend much more than France which itself spends considerably more than West Germany. Britain spends a smaller proportion of total government expenditure on the military and also has smaller armed forces than the other three, but with its professional armed forces it has chosen a capital-intensive posture with higher spending per member of the armed forces.

On the basis of these figures one could argue: first, that it is impossible to compare Britain with its two major EEC partners because of problems of exchange rates, prices and definitions; second, that the British military effort is smaller (military personnel or share of total government spending); third, that it is greater (share of GNP or spending *per capita*) or, fourth, that it is about the same (total expenditure). Different measures produce different rankings because of differences in economic output, population size, total government spending and decisions about the military posture. What matters is to be precise about what question is being asked and then to select the appropriate measure.

For comparing the military effort, the most appropriate measures are total spending, the share of GDP or GNP and spending per head of the population. The other three measures in Table 1.4 tell us more about the structure of government and the detail of the military effort than about its gross magnitude. It should also be remembered that these comparisons of military effort are not the same as a comparison of military capabilities. Finally, Table 1.4 shows that the USA's military effort is greater in both absolute and relative terms than that of its three main European allies: a larger proportion of a larger economic output is devoted to the military, with larger spending per head of a larger population.

British military spending

The Conservative government elected in 1979 came to office with a strong commitment to increase British military spending. The target increase it chose was 3 per cent annually in real terms (i.e. after correcting for inflation). This was the level agreed in NATO at American urging in 1977 for a five-year period. The Labour government had agreed with this, but delayed implementing it until 1979. The Conservatives not only inherited Labour's commitment, but also extended it, planning in 1980 to increase real military spending by 3 per cent each year to 1986 and by 1 per cent thereafter.[6]

Even without the Falklands burden, this budgeting framework is full of problems. It will only be possible to keep to it in one of two contexts. Either the government must persuade or coerce the British people into accepting that the military should take much higher proportions of GDP, or the economy must free itself in one bound from its current profound malaise. The first alternative would have all kinds of extremely unpleasant economic, social and political consequences; the second alternative is extremely unlikely.

But even were the Conservative government to spend what it has planned, Britain's forces cannot be sustained in their present shape because of chronic problems of increasing costs. This was the meaning of the defence review conducted in 1981. As we shall see, this review is but the most recent of a series since the end of the Second World War. As we shall also see, it has done no better than its predecessors in resolving the basic contradictions afflicting British defence policy.

The evolution of the budget

Until 1950, the pattern of British military spending was one of a peacetime plateau, during which about 3 per cent of annual national income was devoted to the military, interspersed by major wartime peaks. Between 1689 and 1945 there were 13 of these peaks, during which more than 6 per cent of annual national income was spent on war; four of these absorbed more than 20 per cent (the War of the Spanish Succession, the Napoleonic Wars and the two World Wars). After each peak, the share of national income devoted to the military took from 5–10 years to descend to the 3 per cent plateau. Although each peak of high spending was associated with a war, wars did not always cause high expenditure. Britain fought numerous wars very cheaply. Lewis Fry Richardson listed 315 wars between 1820 and 1952 in each of which more than 1,000 people were killed; Britain fought in 74 of these, a record of warfare matched by no other country during that period.[7] The low financial cost of most of these wars was the result of Britain's permanent worldwide naval power, which did not need to be augmented in order to be used in combat, and of the pattern of many of Britain's wars in which its professional standing army faced opponents who were technologically less advanced and mounted less firepower. In addition, much of the burden of sustaining the imperial armies was carried by colonial dependants.

After 1945, it appeared at first that the usual descent from the wartime peak to peacetime plateau would happen. During the Second World War, military expenditure absorbed a peak of 60 per cent of national income. This fell off rapidly after the war to 6·5 per cent by 1950. Rearmament at the time of the Korean War took the share up to 10·5 per cent. The Labour government had planned for the share to reach 12 per cent, but supply constraints prevented this from happening and under the Conservative government elected in 1951 a period of defence cuts ensued, bringing the share down to about 7·5 per cent by 1958. From that level, the share fell consistently though unevenly and more slowly, stabilising at around 5 per cent in the 1970s. Identifying the exact level of the share depends, of course, on exactly which measures are used, but all measures indicate that in the 1970s the proportion of national income spent on the military was higher than both the typical peacetime level before 1939 and the proportion devoted to the military by the other western European states.

The cycle of defence reviews

The relative stability in the trends of the military share of GDP has not been produced by accident, nor by government decision alone. It may be seen as a dynamic equilibrium between three influences: first, the strategic aspirations of successive British governments; second, the constraints imposed by Britain's unendingly ailing economy; third, the rising relative costs of providing military goods and services. The interaction of these influences has resulted in a fairly regular cycle of reviews of defence policy. We shall look briefly at the reviews, and then move on to consider these three influences.

The cutbacks in expenditure and forces after the Second World War were followed by dramatic rearmament at the start of the 1950s. New reductions in expenditure began in 1953, and the budget was cut in real terms each year until 1959. The 1957 defence White Paper announced itself as the product of a thorough rethinking of forces and doctrines – the first defence review since rearmament. But except for the termination of conscription, the rethinking was quickly rethought. Most notably, the White Paper had declared the imminent demise of manned aircraft in most military roles, yet by 1959, to stave off the crisis in the aerospace industry resulting from that bold declaration, the TSR-2 aircraft project was begun. The period 1959 to 1964 was one of rising military budgets.

The Labour government elected in 1964 instituted a defence review which lasted until 1966 and whose major casualty was the TSR-2. No sooner was the review completed than another was begun, resulting in the decision to withdraw from 'east of Suez' and to do away with air-craft carriers in the navy. Real military expenditure was falling by the late 1960s, but by then, Britain was partici-pating in an international programme to produce the Multi-Role Combat Aircraft (entering service in 1981 as the Tornado) to fulfil the roles for which the TSR-2 had been designed.

Back in office in 1970, the Conservatives left the 'east of Suez' decision to stand, increased military spending and began a project then known as the 'Through Deck Cruiser' – a ship which looked remarkably like an aircraft carrier. In December 1973 the Conservatives announced reductions in their planned levels of military spending, but this task was actually carried through by Labour, re-elected in 1974 and turning immediately to a further defence review. The result of the review was a plan to stabilise expenditure through the 1970s. On the over-optimistic assumption that the economy would grow at 3 per cent a year, this was expected to reduce the share of GDP spent on the military to something closer to that of the main western European allies. Once again, forces were pulled back from far-flung deployments, and British defence policy moved to a near-total concentration on the commitment to NATO in and around Europe. The Multi-Role Combat Aircraft survived the review; so did the Through Deck Cruiser, but renamed as an Anti-Submarine Warfare (ASW) cruiser.

The 1974 review was followed by a series of further economies until Labour's last defence budget in 1979 increased military spending once more. The Conservatives, returned to power, were concerned with boosting military spending further and, above all, replacing the Polaris force of nuclear-missile-firing submarines. The decision to pur-chase Trident was announced in summer 1980.

Predictable and predicted problems soon surfaced, and it became necessary to trim the planned rate of increase in both annual spending and forces. This was accomplished in the 1981 defence review, where the burden of cuts fell on the navy which lost nine surface warships and was informed it would in the long term have only two instead of three of the new Invincible class ASW Carriers – the second change of name for ships which had started out as Through Deck Cruisers. Invincible itself, the first of this class, was to be sold to Australia. Instead it went to war in the South Atlantic and was reprieved. The Falklands war gave heart to the navy lobby and re-opened all the questions the 1981 review had tried to settle. The war and its aftermath cost about £1 billion in 1982–3, while replacements and the maintenance of fortress Falklands is scheduled to add half a billion a year for the following three financial years. Official figures on Falklands' costs have been as confused and contradictory[8] as official explanations of how Falklands' defence will be fitted into UK strategic planning. British defence policy is back in turmoil.

A simple pattern underlies this apparent chaos. It begins with the specification of strategic and tactical roles which the government aims to fulfil with particular numbers, types and deployments of personnel and equipment. These plans seem feasible only because the resources available in the future are overestimated while the growth in costs is underestimated. The plans proceed until it becomes clear that rising costs and poor economic performance mean the Ministry of Defence cannot meet all the commitments. The response is a short-term economy drive which puts penny-pinching restrictions on stocks of spare parts, maintenance and repairs, practice, living conditions, and so on. This produces a small reduction in costs, but a large reduction in military capability and, while it leaves the major roles and weapons projects untouched, causes tensions and discontent within the armed forces. All this short-term response manages to do, however, is postpone the evil day until a crisis in policy produces a new defence review. In this the order of battle is trimmed, roles are sacrificed and one or two major weapons projects may be scrapped. The casualties of past reviews – the TSR-2, aircraft carriers, foreign bases – are forever mourned by the services who neither forgive nor forget and who, in the fullness of time, often manage to undermine such decisions. Faced with intractable dilemmas, each review compromises rather than resolves, and so the cycle begins all over again.

One of the results of this process is that Britain maintains 'balanced forces'. This is so in two senses. Each service consumes a roughly equal proportion of the budget. At the same time, each service covers a wide range of combat missions. The principle of 'balanced forces' can also be understood as the concept of 'equal misery': each time the hatchet falls, each service manages to ensure that the other two share equally in the misery. But with the 1981 defence review, this principle was qualified: the navy bore the brunt of the tragedy. However, prior to the Falklands action, this could be regarded as only fair, since in 1980 the decision had been taken to purchase Trident missiles and submarines at a cost which is not yet clear, but which is probably in the range of £10–12 billion at 1982 prices. In the end, the structure of the budget owes more to the relative bureaucratic and political clout of the services than it does to strategic calculation.

The dynamics of budgeting

It is widely agreed that the cycle of defence reviews interspersed with short-term economy drives causes erratic planning and inefficient allocation of available resources. Yet the difficulties caused by the conflict between aspirations inherited from an imperial past and the economic realities of the present are virtually taken for granted as a fact of life by defence planners.

Each defence review has seen the shedding of a further element of Britain's imperial military heritage. In the 1981 defence review, it was not far-flung bases but the surface navy which was cut. Although the extent to which an ocean-going navy is related to the imperial past was revealed when virtually the whole surface navy sailed off to war with Argentina in 1982, the cut in its strength in 1981 indicated that future reviews will have to find cuts in the four roles which are the main consumers of the budget. These roles are, first, to maintain the semi-independent 'strategic' nuclear force of Polaris submarines, to be replaced by Trident. In the 1970s, Polaris took a small proportion of the budget, but in the 1980s the purchase of Trident will take a very large slice of the funds available for new weapons production. The second role is the deployment of land and air forces in West Germany; and the third is keeping up the naval presence in the eastern Atlantic and Channel areas where Britain provides around 70 per cent of NATO forces. These two latter roles are the main form of the commitment to NATO as far as British forces and the budget are concerned. The fourth role is to defend Britain itself, which is also the defence of Britain as a base for US nuclear weapons and a staging post for US reinforcements to Europe.

The provision of forces in these roles is geared to government perceptions of the threat from the USSR. But these perceptions are imprecise enough to leave great scope for reducing or altering forces from time to time, irrespective of changes in Soviet forces and deployments.

British forces have been in action almost constantly since the end of the Second World War, in parts of the world far removed from the NATO front with the Warsaw Pact countries. This has provided combat experience in wars utterly unlike the one envisaged by British military planning and has cost many lives. Apart from the Falklands conflict, such war experience has added relatively little to the military budget, since the forces involved would have been maintained in any case and were, in most cases, operating from permanent bases. The high cost of conflict in Northern Ireland is felt on the civil rather than the military account. Future involvement in wars in the third world, however, would be much more expensive and the cost could escalate rapidly if they required large-scale transport and led to the establishment of new bases.

Relative to the four major roles, the domestic activities of the military – 'aid to the civil power' such as strike-breaking, co-operating with the police against 'subversion', storming an embassy and helping to establish the Home Defence system for nuclear and other emergencies – are fairly inexpensive.

Next to the major roles, the second main influence on the budget is the rising real cost of providing military goods and services. As the years pass, even after correcting for inflation, the same amount of money buys less. On average, the prices of all military goods and services in Britain have risen about 2 per cent faster than the general rate of inflation, but in some sectors the difference is much greater. Major equipment prices have risen 6–10 per cent faster, and while price increases for military electronics have outstripped general inflation, the price of civil electronics has actually fallen. The pressure this puts on the budget has been neatly illustrated by a calculation which showed that, based on a simple extrapolation of long-lasting trends, by the year 2036 the entire US military budget would be able to afford but a single combat aircraft.[9] Needless to add, this is not a prediction, merely an illustration of a pressing problem faced by the armed forces of all the industrialised countries.

The key to this process is the increased sophistication of each successive generation of weapon systems. The essential rationale for purchasing a new aircraft is that it will be better than the one it is replacing. In the absence of technological breakthroughs, increasingly marginal variations on a theme increase sophistication only at vastly increased cost. As military technologies become more mature, the cost of even a small improvement grows exponentially.

Once established, the process is self-reinforcing. Increased costs mean, for example, that fewer types of aircraft can be purchased; thus, each type must be capable of doing all the jobs previously done by several specialised types. For this, the new aircraft requires new capabilities which push up costs yet further. The classic example of this process is the multi-role multi-national Tornado now entering service in Britain, Italy and West Germany. It is to be both a bomber and an air defence interceptor, and was at one time planned for air-to-air dog-fighting and close support of ground forces as well, though these two roles seem to have been quietly dropped.

There are many levels of irony in the process. The increasing cost of modern weapons systems means fewer can be purchased. Multi-role capabilities usually mean no single task can be accomplished as effectively as by a specialised system. In addition, increased sophistication reduces reliability (because of the proliferation of complex components) and increases maintenance requirements; all of which adds up to the fact that 'improvement' reduces capability. The process has aptly been dubbed 'baroque'.[10]

The pressure of increasing costs evidently means that the continued ability to fulfil roles requires more resources to be made available. But the resources available to the military effort are constrained by the rate of growth of the economy and the share of national income which can be devoted to it. From the end of the Second World War British GDP grew by about 2·5 per cent annually; among advanced capitalist countries, only the USA's economy grew as slowly. Between 1973 and 1979 the annual British growth rate dropped to about 1 per cent; since 1979 it has stopped completely. Growth rates fell elsewhere after 1973 but Britain's relative position – growing at half the average for advanced capitalist economies – stayed the same. Inevitably, poor economic performance restricts the resources available for defence. Moreover, increasing the proportion of GDP spent on the military can only be a palliative, since resources are then diverted from investment, which reduces the rate of growth yet further.[11] Indeed, one of the proximate causes for Britain's relatively poor economic performance over the past three decades has been the diversion of resources away from civil industry into the military effort at the time of the Korean war rearmament.[12] Diverting resources into the military sector may relieve economic constraints in the short term, but will make them much worse in the long term.

The cycle of defence reviews and the pattern of chops and changes which underlies the relative stability of British defence budgeting are the effects of the scissor blades of rising costs and economic inadequacy trimming strategic aspirations.

Constraints on the budget

In looking at the effects of these pressures, it is useful to think in terms of three factors: resource, allocative and stabilisation constraints.

Resource constraints refer to physical resources (materials, plant, people) mobilised by military spending. Such constraints may be imposed by the increased international price or diminishing availability of raw materials. They may also be the result of gaps in industrial capacity. For example, the commitment to build British nuclear-powered submarines to carry US Trident missiles will absorb Britain's industrial capacity for making nuclear-powered submarines because only one yard in the country (in Barrow) is regarded as suitable for such work. So when the 1981 defence review announced a 'shift in emphasis' towards submarines, it did not mean more submarines would be built – rather, it meant surface ships would be reduced. Similarly, in the USA, the rearmament programme begun by President Carter and continuing under the Reagan administration is hampered by a lack of industrial capacity in key sectors.[13]

Allocative constraints refer to the limitations on overall spending imposed by the operation of social, economic and political factors. Military spending is but one demand on the public purse and on national income. The level of military spending is set as a result of competition between different priorities – other government spending, private consumption, investment – asserted in the complex interplay of strengths between and within the various social classes. The pattern of allocation reflects their social strength and political clout, the alliances and compromises which the various groups make, and the economic context in which they operate. This competition does not start afresh each year, beginning with a clean slate; the pattern of allocative preferences is established over the long term and is relatively stable. It is usually possible to accomplish short-term shifts in the pattern only at the margins and on a relatively small scale.

The stabilisation constraint can be thought of as an imperative. When planned expenditure outruns feasible expenditure, a stabilisation of policy is the enforced result; in Britain, the moment of stabilisation is called a defence review. For long-term stability in actual military expenditure, which is the restated goal of every defence review, spending plans must accord with long-term allocative patterns and feasible economic performance. If this imperative is ignored, either allocative preferences must be changed or the stabilisation constraint makes itself felt. The cycle of defence reviews results from the inability of successive governments to give due respect to this imperative. Typically, this lack of respect has been expressed in over-optimistic assumptions about economic performance, exacerbated by underestimating costs. The Thatcher government, however, has shown its disrespect by making stringent demands on the overall allocation of resources.

We can get an idea of what this means by comparing plans for military spending in the 1980s with the pattern hitherto. The plan to increase real spending by 3 per cent a year to 1986, and 1 per cent thereafter, must be implemented in a period in which the government estimated that the economy would grow by 1 per cent a year. This would put the military share of GDP at about 6 per cent in the mid-1980s, and would thus mean making increased resources available by withdrawing them from elsewhere – other public spending, private consumption or investment. Moreover, the assumption of 1 per cent economic growth, taken from the government's Medium Term Financial Strategy, could be an overestimate, which means the military share of GDP would be even higher. Military spending from the early 1950s to the 1970s is well explained by an equation which relates the share of British GDP spent on the military to growth in GDP, the relative price effect (i.e. the difference between military and civil costs) and the size of the annual US and Soviet budgets (as estimated).[14] Assuming 1 per cent growth in British GDP, 3 per cent growth in the US military budget and 4 per cent perceived growth in the Soviet budget, together with a 2 per cent relative price effect (the recent average) provides a reasonable set of inputs for applying this economic model to the 1980s.

The result is straightforward: if those past allocative patterns were to hold in the 1980s, British real military spending would decline over the decade by an average of 1·5 per cent a year and the share of GDP going to the military would fall by a couple of decimal points. The gap between real increases of 3 per cent a year and real reductions of 1·5 per cent a year indicates the scale of shifts in macro-economic resource allocation that the Conservatives must accomplish to fulfil their military spending plans.

We do not know if it will be possible to make these shifts. They can only be made at enormous social and economic cost, imposing large cuts in other spending programmes, structurally weakening the economy yet further by consuming investment resources, effectively constructing a dual sector economy in which the military sector booms for a while and the civil sector stagnates. There is likely to be powerful political opposition to such shifts, which would have to be met by either coercion or the creation of a war psychology, or both. Yet all of this would still not solve the military's problems, would still not be enough to maintain forces of the current size and range of missions, equipped with the most modern weaponry.

If these shifts are not made, the prospect is a confrontation with the stabilisation constraint, that is, there will be a crisis in defence policy followed by a review. If that review obeyed the imperative of stability, it would lead to a fundamental restructuring of British military policy and forces; if not, it will be a matter of counting the years until the next-review-but-one comes round.

In the end, the prospects and shape of policy and the size of the budget will be decided through political struggle. If those shifts in allocation are not made it will be because of mobilised political resistance, because the people who make up the abstract social forces we have been discussing refuse to put up with those changes and the demands they make of them, refuse to be frightened and refuse to be sucked into a war psychology.

2. The drive to militarism

There are numerous accounts of how the military expenditure of any state is determined, of how and why a particular level of spending is set, of what purposes it serves. The orthodox account imagines a rational state conducting a cost-benefit analysis. The costs, often referred to as resource or opportunity costs, are the civilian goods and services which are forgone as a result of military spending. The benefits are usually described as increased security (though this term merits a scrutiny as careful as that given the numbers). The theory says that military spending should be increased if the benefits outweigh the economic costs. Within this theoretical framework, debates are then conducted about the measurement of costs and benefits, with one school arguing that military spending provides economic as well as strategic benefits.

Opposing this account are several others which emphasise such things as the momentum of technology, the operation of military bureaucracies and industrial interests, the role of military spending in maintaining profitability and economic growth, or merely politicians' desires to be re-elected. All these theories tend to reject the image of the state as a rational actor and to identify domestic forces as the major determinants of military spending.

Each of these accounts contains elements of the truth, but each alone is too limited in scope. Our approach begins by recognising that capitalism as an international system faces certain strategic needs to which capitalist states must respond to ensure the conditions under which the system can continue. This response is complicated by the differing needs of individual states and uneven economic development among capitalist countries. Similarly, the communist states face certain strategic needs to which they too must respond.

To speak of the state responding to needs and taking action is to speak loosely. The state is not a unitary actor. It is a set of institutions which provides an arena for conflict out of which come the decisions shaping military spending. The economic and political power of capital in western societies means that the requirements of capitalism constrain state action and dominate decisions. But capital is not a single bloc. Within nations and internationally, different groups of capitalists have different and possibly competing requirements. There is a relative separation of the state from both capital and individual capitalists. The interests of the politicians and bureaucrats who operate the state apparatus, the representations of the arms makers and the demands of the working class will all have some influence. In the case of military spending, the most influential grouping is the military–industrial complex – that confluence of interests between arms manufacturers and the military establishment. But, again, the military–industrial complex is not an homogeneous bloc. Differences of emphasis and conflicts of interest abound, among the manufacturers, between them and the services and civilian bureaucracy, and among the services and bureaucracy. This grouping is also constrained by the strategic needs of capital and by other political and economic forces, and is thus not an independent determinant of military spending. But it does act as a crucial transmission mechanism, shaping the way strategic needs are met, translating them into decisions and programmes. We discuss it and its role in the next chapter.

Strategic requirements

Noting these qualifications about the complexity of state decision-making, we shall now look at the broad framework of strategic requirements for military spending. This framework does not of itself explain why or how particular forces have been deployed or particular weapons systems purchased. It simply sets a context within which these more detailed questions can be asked. We shall look first at the advanced capitalist states and then at the USSR and its allies, using a similar framework in the two cases. We do not consider the less developed countries, because they are extremely heterogeneous and broad generalisations are likely to be misleading.

Advanced capitalism

We have found it useful to consider the issue in terms of four dimensions of strategic requirement, four arenas in which armed force has a part to play. First, the capitalist states as a group must defend the international capitalist system from the threat posed to it by established communist states. Second, armed force is an integral part of the mechanisms by which relations between the advanced capitalist states and the less developed countries are regulated. Third, military power is the basis of a hegemonic state's ability to organise the system so that it can contain and constrain rivalries between capitalist states. Fourth, a state's monopoly of armed force and its ability to mobilise militaristic and patriotic sentiment insures against internal threats to the existing social order.

Behind the rhetoric of cold war, it is perfectly realistic for the administration of a capitalist state to perceive communism as a threat and to make military preparations against it. Furthermore, the integration of capitalism as a world system makes it realistic for various states to attempt to co-ordinate their preparations through an international organisation like NATO. This does not mean that policies, even within an alliance, will be uniform. Differences in capabilities and interests will produce different emphases in policy together with some major divergences – for example, the neutral capitalist states in Europe.

Military relations with less developed countries involve supporting client regimes (and 'clientising' as many regimes as possible) as well as countering social and political movements which challenge western interests. Even when they are not in government, the military in less developed countries tend to be a major conduit for the transmission of ideology and power relations to those societies, a mechanism which is maintained and extended through the supply of arms, training and advisers. Since the Second World War, the third world has been the scene of almost continuous conflict. Regional hostilities and anti-imperialist struggles have become enmeshed in superpower confrontation, generating a series of bloody wars in Africa, Asia and the Middle East. Indeed, this dimension of the requirement for military expenditure is widely seen (e.g. by Reagan and Thatcher) as inextricable from the first, as the third world becomes the arena for superpower conflict, and raw materials from less developed countries gain in strategic significance.

Since the Second World War, the USA's 'nuclear umbrella' over the other advanced capitalist states and its capacity for global military intervention have been major supports in its hegemonic position. The participation of other capitalist states in a US-led alliance has confirmed their participation in the system and acceptance of US hegemony. In western Europe after 1945, Marshall Aid from the USA was a major factor in economic reconstruction, while NATO, dominated and underwritten by the USA, was a crucial feature of political reconstruction. The USA's ability and willingness to use force to deal with challenges to the system it represented both ensured the cohesion of the system and, reinforcing the USA's economic leverage, strengthened its leading position. While it maintained this role effectively during the 1950s and 1960s it gained substantial advantages over other capitalist states, but the long-term costs were large. Under the umbrella of American power, most other capitalist states did not need to arm themselves so intensively and could therefore devote resources to investment and growth, increasing Japanese and western European economic power against the USA – ultimately threatening US hegemony, and thus the system it guaranteed. In this respect, with the remnants of an imperial role and then an imperial self-image, Britain was the major exception to the rule and its economic benefits were thus less.

In domestic politics, armed forces have a dual role. Emphasising military values may develop feelings of national identity, prestige and sovereignty, and perhaps also the values of discipline, obedience to authority and respect for hierarchy. The power of the Falklands factor in UK politics is a recent illustration of the ideological strength of military values. In addition, the reality and the mythology of conflict between capitalism and communism can be used to moderate internal threats to the existing order and isolate opposition groups. These effects constitute the ideological role. Furthermore, in its coercive role, armed force is the ultimate guarantor of state power. The military can be used both to break strikes and run essential services during strikes, and in case of need are available for open war against a direct and violent internal threat.

Within this fourfold framework, the requirement for high military expenditure in the post-war period can be explained in terms of the threats to international capitalism from a variety of sources – from rival social systems in eastern Europe and Asia; from anti-imperialist movements in subjugated countries; from a possible repetition of the inter-imperialist rivalries and economic conflict up to 1939; and from actual and potential class and race conflict in the advanced capitalist societies.

The Soviet system

A similar framework is applicable in the case of communist states. It is certainly reasonable for the USSR to feel threatened by the advanced capitalist states in a whole range of ways. In the case of China, we should remember that for two decades the USA was unable even to admit the existence of the People's Republic. Sino-Soviet rivalry, however, is something different: there is no parallel to it among the advanced capitalist countries. But what is at stake in the military element of that rivalry is familiar – the question of hegemony, of maintaining and regulating a group of states with similar social systems. The Soviet hold in eastern Europe is very much a function of its armed strength, while China's armed forces provide much of the guarantee against its inclusion in the Soviet bloc.

In relations with poorer countries the USSR has for the past two decades used the indirect levers of military strength (naval visits, arms aid and exports, training and advisers) to secure and maintain influence. More recently, it has equipped and supported Cuban forces in Angola and Ethiopia and used its own armed forces in the invasion of Afghanistan. Finally, to retain domestic social and political cohesion, the USSR has as much need as advanced capitalist states, and possibly more, for both the ideology of militarism and the potential for direct military coercion.

The basic framework of Soviet strategic requirements for military spending is thus analogous to that of advanced capitalist states. However, among states which call themselves socialist, ruled by parties which call themselves communist, there is not the same acceptance as there is among capitalist states of an international system of regulation. The Sino-Soviet conflict is rooted in Chinese rejection of a Soviet international socialist system. The wars between China and Vietnam and between Vietnam and Kampuchea are symptomatic of this same lack of regulation. The situation in eastern Europe notwithstanding, relations between these states are not conducted in a context as orderly as relations between advanced capitalist states.

International militarism

The four dimensions of the strategic requirement for military spending interact with each other. The confrontation between West and East is not only a real confrontation, but also an ideological construct which helps legitimise military intervention in the third world, rationalise the organising role of the hegemonic power, and maintain national cohesion and discipline. The result is that the confrontation between the superpowers, with their respective allies, has become self-reproducing: for a variety of reasons, it is useful for advanced capitalist states to have this Soviet enemy, and therefore useful to step up the confrontation both through rhetoric and through deploying new weapons. Over the past three decades, whatever the fluctuations in the details of each side's behaviour and the relations between them, armed confrontation has been a constant. Indeed, the momentum of the armament process, based on the political, military and industrial institutions which fuel it, has become self-generating. If one could argue that political confrontation between the superpowers produced military confrontation, it now seems as if the military dimension has taken the confrontation over entirely. Competitive armament processes on each side are a major determinant forcing continued confrontation. Edward Thompson has neatly summarised this process and its potential consequences in all their irrationality as 'exterminist',[1] yet it is also important to understand how this apparently crazed and addictive process of armed confrontation serves certain definite functions.

The capitalist state provides those conditions necessary for capital accumulation that cannot be provided by individual capitalists. These include the maintenance of appropriate social relations, sustained by legal and monetary systems which enable circulation to proceed smoothly, and the provision and regulation of the supply of necessary labour power and raw materials. The nation state can act directly to meet these needs for national capital, but for international trade and finance to proceed, these needs must also be met at a world level. The growing internationalisation of capital, the advancing integration of capitalism as a world system and the increasing complexity of the system, all intensify the need for international regulation. In the nineteenth century, when most production took place within nations, the organisational requirements of capital were much simpler than they are today.

There is no world state. Individual capitalist states have

different requirements and competing interests. As a result of this absence and this disunity, the functions of international regulation tend to be performed by a single nation state which has economic, political and military predominance. Coercion and influence enable this state to hold a position of hegemony. Britain took this role before the First World War. The USA assumed it after the Second World War, and in so doing it created the strategic and political basis for the long boom in the capitalist world economy from 1950 to 1974.[2] The length and severity of the economic slump between the two World Wars was partly the consequence of the lack of a hegemonic power, Britain being incapable of taking this role and the USA being unwilling.

The period in which the USA moved into a conscious adoption of the hegemonic role is also the period of the launching of the cold war with the USSR. The cold war, a conscious strategy for relations with the USSR, was based on the political assumption that conflict between the USA and the USSR was inevitable and irreducible. American interests in Europe, eastern Asia and elsewhere were seen to be fundamentally in conflict with what were perceived to be Soviet interests. This assumption laid the basis in the USA for political support for assuming the costs of being a global policeman. In other countries, it laid the basis for accepting the USA's leading role in organising the system in return for the strength of its protection against the Soviet 'threat'. The cold war and the post-1945 reorganisation of international capitalism, including economic and political reconstruction in the defeated and war-torn countries, went hand in hand.

By the late 1960s, US dominance was in decline. Low growth of output and productivity in the USA made it less important as a supplier and a market; the glut of dollars on the international money market drove down the value of the dollar, undermined US policy and finally eliminated the dollar-based system of international exchange rates constructed after the Second World War. These economic and currency problems were in part a consequence of the high military spending, foreign investment and foreign military deployment associated with the USA's hegemonic role. One symptom of this loss of economic dominance was that whereas the GDP of the US in 1953 was twice that of Britain, France, Italy, Japan and West Germany combined, by 1977 it was less than the combined GDPs of these five countries. Under US hegemony the system had worked so well, especially for Japan and West Germany, that it finally became unworkable.

Corresponding to this was a loss of military dominance, symbolised by defeat in Vietnam and by Soviet attainment of strategic nuclear parity (understood as the ability of each to blow up the other several times over). The 1973 oil crisis and general increase in oil prices from 1974, revealed US impotence in the face of OPEC, a well-organised cartel of suppliers of a crucial raw material.

The decline in US hegemony thus relates to three of the four elements in the general framework of requirements for military spending. Although the extent and growth of Soviet armed strength is regularly exaggerated in the West for propaganda purposes, it is evident that it did grow consistently and relatively steadily from the mid-1960s in all categories.[3] At the same time, the difficulties of enforcing subordination on certain key, less developed, countries were overwhelming, while regulation of relations between advanced capitalist countries was fading. The economic problems growing from and exacerbating this relative lack of regulation threatened also to sharpen class conflict within the advanced capitalist countries. These economic problems are well known – volatile exchange rates, the debt defaults, low growth, growing protectionism. These symptoms are very similar to those produced in the 1930s by lack of regulation.

In this environment, the need for capitalism to re-establish regulation is pressing. It is therefore no surprise to be faced by a new cold war. In broad terms, there appear to be two possible outcomes for relations within advanced capitalism. Either the USA could restore its hegemony, or the capitalist world could fragment into regional trading blocs (such as a more unified EEC) with regulation within them and conflict between them. The new cold war is one element in a strategy to prevent the latter from occurring. It is both a product of the disintegration of US hegemony – an often hysterical reaction to the uncertainties, feelings of vulnerability and economic disruptions this has produced – and a basis for creating renewed US hegemony.

In the USA's eyes, the problem facing the West is lack of leadership and lack of readiness to accept leadership. The response has been to counterbalance political and economic decline by a reinvigorated military effort. This is very much the programme advocated by an important 1979 *Business Week* article.[4] At the same time, the other capitalist states have to be pushed into increasing their own military spending and reconfirming their ties with the USA. In this process, the image of a looming and omnipresent Soviet threat becomes a crucial instrument of propaganda and ideology.

There is some objective basis for this strategy. Despite a relative decline, the USA remains the largest national capitalist economy. It has immense military capacity, both nuclear and conventional, on which most other advanced capitalist states predicate their defence policies. There is no single rival to the USA for hegemony. Working from this basis, the USA, first under Carter and now more spectacularly under Reagan, has both urged its allies to increase military spending and planned an immense build-up of its own, outstripping even the increases in spending for the war in Vietnam.[5]

The difficulties of this strategy are twofold. Firstly, the problems it seeks to solve are profound. It is not clear that state leaderships in the other advanced capitalist countries will be willing to identify the health of the international economy with the position of the USA and subordinate their own interests accordingly. It is not clear that political consent for the various elements of the strategy will be either forthcoming or durable; and even if consent is gained, increasing military spending will exacerbate economic weaknesses. Secondly, it is an extremely dangerous strategy.

Its central military element demands that all problems be seen as military problems, or at least amenable to military solutions, and the Soviet hand will always be identified in there somewhere. Such an approach could easily lead to wars that are very costly in terms of both money and lives; and it could lead on to nuclear holocaust.

The functions of the new cold war are essentially the same as the old one: to maintain the cohesion necessary to offset rivalries between advanced capitalist states, re-strengthen the hold on poorer countries, outface the USSR, and provide an ideological base from which to attack working-class militancy. Just as firm domestic discipline was necessary to raise the rate of exploitation and generate rapid economic growth after the Second World War, so it is necessary once again, now the period of rapid growth is over. But this highly functional new cold war presents dangers which are, if anything, greater than those in the old cold war.

Domestic militarism

Ideologies cannot be manipulated at will by the state, the ruling class or the mass media. Ideologies – the ways in which we understand ourselves, our environment and our place within it – grow from experience and education in the widest sense. They are not therefore easily amenable to propagandistic fine-tuning and, like our lives, carry no inherent logical consistency. Nonetheless, time and again, it has been possible for a deliberate and sustained effort by a ruling class to change the ways in which large numbers of people think about certain crucial aspects of their lives, their environment and their place within it – in other words, to affect elements of their ideologies in politically important ways. Militarism has proven to have a particularly powerful ideological pull.

The First World War provides perhaps the classic example. Before the war, the continental European socialist parties of the Second International had understood the possibility of inter-imperialist war. They had agreed workers should not kill each other for the profit of respective ruling classes, that their enemies were not each other but imperialist and militarist states and ruling classes. In August 1914 only small minorities of the French and German socialist parties stood by those views, and they were as bitterly reviled by their erstwhile comrades as by their governments. Britain, in 1914, faced a militant women's suffrage movement, a militant syndicalist workers' mass movement and a revolt within the ruling classes and army over Irish independence. With the war, most of the suffrage movement abandoned activism for the duration, working-class men joined the forces in massive numbers (so that conscription had to be introduced to regulate the influx and retain workers in key industries), and the ruling class agreed a truce over Ireland.

Clearly, the element of patriotism is a major factor. But patriotic fervour is itself largely a construct of the military tradition. In Britain, it is the memory of victories over the Spanish Armada, at Blenheim, Waterloo and Rorke's Drift, and in the two World Wars, which take pride of place in summoning up the patriotic spirit – not memories of innovative industrialisation or the railway boom in the nineteenth century.

Moreover, the values which patriotism demands and inspires are contained within the military tradition: discipline, respect for authority, obedience and self-sacrifice when called for – whether to die in battle or desist from strikes for the duration (of the war or the economic crisis). More recently, a further virtue has been added to the list – military efficiency.

It is probably fruitless to point out that military efficiency is a concept embodying a good deal of mythology; that all wars have involved a waste of human lives inefficient even by the criterion of winning the war; that the history of military technology is a history of poor production, slovenly maintenance and regular breakdowns; that the most effective armed forces have often been those in which rigid hierarchies were broken down somewhat to allow initiative from below.

The values embraced in militarist ideology have taken on their own life and their own laws.

Debunking the mythology of the ideology, however, should not detract attention from its enormous pull. At its crudest core it connotes obedience to the nation-state, the efficient fulfilment of the nation-state's requirements and identification with its objectives. These demands are elevated above any social or political loyalty which might move in a different direction. Accompanied by an identified external threat to the interests and objectives of the nation-state, it becomes a potent and pervasive force. Three specific examples indicate the ways in which it can work.

At the onset of the first cold war, McCarthyism was effectively a coercive force for the organisation of American opinion. It purged dissidence among the elite and outlawed socialism among the masses. It fractured working-class politics and mobilised the trade unions in the service of the cold war. Its basic reference points were the external threat from the USSR and its conscious and unconscious accomplices within American society. Although McCarthy himself had to be dumped and discredited for 'going too far', the ideology he was identified with successfully disciplined opinion and equipped it with a duty: to identify, resist and vilify the threat within and without.

In West Germany in the 1970s, the *Berufsverbot* regulations were used to ban from government jobs those who held opinions defined as contrary to the Federal Republic's constitution. It was used not only against people in government ministries and positions sensitive from the point of view of security, but also, for example, against postal workers and, especially, teachers. Like McCarthyism it was used against socialists and liberals alike, was predicated on the need to resist the dual internal/external threat from the USSR and was a coercive instrument to regulate opinion.

A third example is Thatcherism in Britain in the 1970s. When Margaret Thatcher was elected as party leader in 1975, the Conservatives were stunningly disunited on virtually every issue of social and economic policy. The only policy which commanded general agreement was the criticism of the Labour government for cutting military spending (or, more accurately, for refusing to increase it) and the consequent need to increase military spending when the Conservatives returned to office. A series of militantly anti-Soviet speeches in 1975 served not only to express the policy, but also as a rallying cry for party unity. Her authoritarian populism enabled the Conservatives not only to win the election, but to exploit the Falklands affair three years later. Imperial nostalgia, images of war, and dreams of sovereignty divided the opposition and mobilised the public.

The effects of these ideological campaigns are not uniform. They are not guaranteed to succeed. Rather, they mark out sites for continuing ideological and political struggles.

Modern states have tended to maintain a distinction between military activities and policing. The former have been reserved for external enemies, the latter for criminality. In the face of rebellion and civil war this distinction naturally breaks down, but it has also been modified in most states to face three other kinds of challenge.

Some strikes are seen as a threat to the fundamental well-being of state and society. Where they have the technical capabilities, armed forces can be mobilised to run essential services, thus reducing the impact of the strike and the bargaining power of the strikers. In other cases, troops can be called upon to break strikes and occupations forcefully.

Second, there is the question of public order and disorder. Many states maintain 'paramilitary' forces to supplement or replace regular police for dealing with riots and policing large demonstrations. In other states, such as the UK, either the army can be called directly on to the streets (as in Northern Ireland), or the way in which the police handle disturbances becomes increasingly militarised in both equipment and tactics (as in mainland Britain in 1981).

Finally, there is the question of political opposition, especially movements which do not stay within the bounds of parliamentary electoralism. State intelligence services which are supposed to be combating foreign spies develop files on left-wing parties and political activists, and, occasionally, with less enthusiasm, on the far right as well. At the same time, police agencies divert their attention away from criminality and maintain files on the same parties and activists. When the system becomes properly efficient, police and counter-intelligence contribute material to the same computerised files. The result is that certain opposition groups come to be identified by the state as both criminal and agents of a foreign power.

What is happening in all these cases, whether the army takes on police roles, or the police begin to look more like an army, or a paramilitary force is created, is that the policing function is being militarised. The interlocking ideological effects of militarism seep through the state apparatus as well as the populace.

Soviet militarism

Afghanistan

Soviet armed forces invaded Afghanistan at the end of 1979. The drama of this event has been multiplied several times by eager propagandists in the West, but even without their efforts the invasion raises crucial issues about armed force in Soviet politics and policy. But in taking the invasion as the sensitive starting point for considering these issues it is necessary to begin by untangling the propaganda from the basic issues.

Despite official statements in the West, the invasion did not start the new cold war or kill detente. Detente was already being eroded by a series of niggling actions in US–Soviet diplomacy in 1977 and 1978. It was under pressure in the USA in 1976 when, during the presidential election campaign, President Ford dropped the term 'detente' from his political vocabulary to head off pressure from his right in the form of Ronald Reagan. NATO's decision to increase military spending all round by 3 per cent annually was taken in 1977. Also in 1977 the process began which resulted in 1979 in the decision to deploy cruise and Pershing II missiles to western Europe – a decision finally taken about a fortnight before the invasion of Afghanistan.

The Soviet invasion, then, is not alone responsible for the erosion of detente. But it may have reflected a decision by the Soviet leadership that detente was no longer of supreme importance. The most casual glance at American politics in 1979 would have indicated the likely response to a Soviet invasion of another country, even one in which the USA had precious few interests and of whose whereabouts most Americans were probably unaware.

At the same time, the invasion reveals a Soviet readiness to use armed force that is different from the invasions of Hungary in 1956 and Czechoslovakia in 1968. Both those invasions were actions within the Soviet bloc system. The case of Afghanistan represents the first time since the Second World War that the USSR has risked large forces in actual combat outside its universally accepted 'sphere of influence'. Hitherto the USSR has been much more cautious than the USA about armed intervention in another country's affairs. The invasion of Afghanistan may represent a watershed.

The USSR's own explanation that it was invited in by the legitimate government cannot explain why the head of that government had to be killed. But to some extent the invasion is a 'policing' action similar to previous actions in Hungary and Czechoslovakia. 'Aiding' the state means changing its leadership. Before Soviet forces went in, Soviet advisers were present in Afghanistan, attached to every government department, exercising profound influence. The government faced widespread dissent, especially from the rural population. The Soviet response to these problems appears to have been to stiffen the fight against rural resistance by getting more involved itself, at the same time ensuring it had a compliant government in Afghanistan. In that process of profound influence followed by large armed forces, the USSR's actions in Afghanistan show some similarities with the USA's in Vietnam in the early 1960s. The inability of military force to provide a quick 'solution' to social and political problems suggests further similarities with Vietnam.

Internal militarism

Recourse to military means in Afghanistan must have been highly tempting to a state for which the military issue has always loomed large. While one can point to a large number of Soviet disarmament proposals made by the USSR since 1945, it would be pointless and ridiculous to ignore the strong military dimension to Soviet politics and policies.

We have already shown how difficult it is to have any accurate figure for the proportion of economic output devoted to the military in the USSR. A common estimate is 10–12 per cent. This is much higher than the current norm in advanced capitalist countries; and it is a higher proportion of an output which is lower per head of the population.

This high military share of output can be understood in terms of the fourfold strategic framework discussed earlier. In particular, it seems clear that official ideology coheres around a set of values based on discipline, patriotism and the role of Soviet armed forces in 'defending socialism'. It appears that there is a highly systematic attempt to inculcate a military and patriotic ethos among school students.[6] Within such an ethos, identifying 'dissidents' as threats to security is quite straightforward. It is the Soviet counterpart of the western temptation to identify militant trade unionists as being in the pay of Moscow. It is, in fact, a reflection of the weak pulling power of official ideology that the USSR cannot tolerate even relatively disorganised and isolated intellectual opposition.

Two further factors, however, are necessary to understand Soviet militarism. The first is the role of the military-industrial institutions; the second is made up of the lessons of Soviet history.

The role of the institutions – research and design bureaux and the industrial production units – is analogous to that of the western military–industrial complex. Of course, there are many important differences: the lack of profit motive; the institutions are all part of the state itself; opportunities for determined political lobbying for sectional interests are more restricted. But in 'the dictated balancing of interests from above' which characterises economic planning in the Soviet bloc,[7] these institutions are tremendously influential.

This stems directly from the USSR's strategic requirement for military expenditure and military industry. But, as in the West, the consequence is a self-reproducing power. The process is one of incremental technological momentum which is to some extent independent of the details of East–West relations. In the past decade, this momentum has shown signs of increasing acceleration as new projects replace old ones showing relatively more innovation with each succeeding weapon system. Soviet military technology is thus becoming increasingly sophisticated and, since the effort is to catch up with US technology, it appears to be following the USA's lead into increasingly 'baroque' realms.

Soviet military industry has proven to be more dynamic and innovative than its civil counterpart. To some extent, this may be traced to the contrast between the contexts in which civil and military industry operate: there is no market mechanism to spur civil innovation, and no substitute for it either; on the other hand, military industry functions in an international strategic environment which is highly competitive. But the greater dynamism on the military side must also be traced to the particular favour with which it is treated, to its priority demands on resources including skilled people.

This favoured treatment is not solely a reflection of the strategic requirement for military expenditure as we have so far stated it. The requirement is refracted through the USSR's historical experience. The Soviet state was born in revolution, civil war and imperialist invasion; the USSR suffered enormously in the war with Germany from 1941. After the Second World War it faced the USA's policy of containment and encirclement. Confrontation with the West has been supplemented by conflict and confrontation with China.

Excessive caution, suspicion, over-insurance and paranoia about threats to Soviet security are not surprising products of that history. Yet perhaps more influential in the long term is that, in the 1920s, the Soviet state, fragile and isolated, set about speedy industrialisation largely in order to develop military industry as a basic necessity for the defence of the USSR. The characteristics of industrialisation produced at that time have never been removed. In a very real sense, the USSR is a warfare economy (with some resemblance to the British economy during the Second World War): central planning is combined with priority for the military effort. Extended over time, this priority has acted as a force for inertia in the civil economy and in the political development of the country. It is hard to say whether the new Soviet leadership will either want or be able to shift away from the warfare economy. It is at least equally likely that the strength of the armament institutions and the pervasiveness of military and patriotic values in the state apparatus will provide strong economic and ideological bases for continuing the present pattern.

The USSR and eastern Europe

The use of Soviet troops in East Berlin in 1953, Hungary in 1956, Czechoslovakia in 1968; and unsubtle hints of their use against Solidarity in Poland before the military clamp-down in December 1981: these events remind us of the importance of armed force in holding the Soviet bloc together.

Indeed, the Soviet bloc was largely created by armed force. It was the fruit of victory for the USSR at the end of the Second World War and recognised as such by at least some western leaders. 'Revolutions' in eastern Europe were made possible and guaranteed by the Soviet army. The positions of Cuba and Vietnam in the Soviet bloc are different. Neither has faced Soviet conquest or occupation; both joined the Council for Mutual Economic Assistance (the members of which constitute the Soviet bloc) only after they were economically isolated by advanced capitalism.

In eastern Europe, the Soviet bloc has shown marked fissiparous tendencies. The Yugoslavian form of socialism proved unacceptable to Stalin, who also found it could be neither subordinated nor intimidated. Albania left the Warsaw Pact in 1968 and the USSR has shown little interest and no capacity for pulling it back in. Romania has developed an independent foreign policy, has no Soviet troops stationed on its territory and strictly limits its participation in Warsaw Pact exercises. In 1978 it went as far as refusing to increase military spending and entertaining Hua Guo-Feng, then Chairman of the Chinese Communist Party. In 1981 it organised major demonstrations opposing both US and Soviet nuclear weapons. There have been economic and political developments against the direction of the bloc as a whole in East Germany, Hungary, Czechoslovakia and Poland. It is widely agreed that non-Soviet Warsaw Pact forces would prove extremely unreliable. Even a NATO invasion of eastern Europe might not galvanise them into being reliable Soviet allies.[8]

All this reveals the weak economic and ideological appeal of Soviet socialism. For some, relatively well-favoured in material terms, the appeal is strong; these are in or close to the economic and political elite. But for the mass of the population, the norm appears to be a passive acceptance of the system, certainly not an enthusiastic allegiance. Domestic repression holds each individual eastern European polity and society together. Soviet armed presence cements the eastern European bloc as a whole. The Soviet leadership continues to believe the bloc is necessary as a buffer zone against the West, and to that end maintains huge armed forces in eastern Europe as a garrison force.

The USSR and the cold war

We have explained both the old and the new cold wars in terms of the requirement for an international system of state regulation within advanced capitalism. The USSR is not a part of this system but it is clearly a part of the cold war. How should this participation be viewed?

It may be tempting to see Soviet involvement in the cold war as that of a potential victim acting in self-defence. There is some basis for this view. Both cold wars can be traced directly to the interests and the actions of advanced capitalist states. The story of the arms race is largely a story of the USSR attempting to catch up. It was the USA which set the pattern of armed intervention in other countries and global naval deployments (following the earlier British example).

But our discussion of the USSR and its bloc suggests it was well suited to play an organic role in the first cold war, developing its bloc system behind a fortress mentality. Today, it is all too easy for the USSR to attempt to deal with fissiparous tendencies in eastern Europe by re-strengthening the fortress. With a warfare economy, powerful military–industrial institutions and a pervasive military presence in society and politics, the USSR and cold war are well suited to each other.

We must therefore reverse the question, and ask whether the USSR, far from being a defensive participant, is inherently aggressive, driven by Marxism–Leninist ideology towards global domination. There are numerous variations on this common western thesis, but the evidence for all of them is exceedingly thin. The basic thesis seems to fit with the acquisition of eastern Europe in the 1940s and the invasion of Afghanistan in 1979. It leaves most Soviet actions in the intervening years unexplained. Its version of Marxism–Leninism is in any case based on an amusingly selective process of quotation from the classic texts and modern political speeches. It has never tried to explain why there should be more continuity from the classic texts (selectively treated) to modern Soviet foreign policy than there is from those texts to modern Soviet society.

Soviet foreign policy can best be explained in terms of a fairly cautious Soviet assessment of how best to meet state interests. Stalin and his successors have always been ready to qualify, reduce or simply terminate support for revolutionary movements whenever the interests of the Soviet state required. Soviet socialism has proven to be far less economically thrusting than capitalism with its unending hunger for new markets, resources and labour. In foreign policy, the USSR has sought above all else to avoid international isolation, which is why it has so eagerly sought influence in the third world. The USSR, then, is a powerful state which primarily seeks to advance its own interests – to maintain its domestic grip, its hold in eastern Europe and its influence among the non-aligned countries. To these ends, it uses armed force both directly and indirectly. But it is not a revolutionary state, either at home or abroad.

Thus, the use of the term 'warfare economy' to characterise the Soviet economy does not imply that the USSR is poised to launch a war or is inherently expansionist. A warfare economy does not necessarily mean a war-mongering state.

There can, however, be little doubt that the USSR has provided a number of useful pegs on which to hang the propaganda of the new cold war. There can be no doubting its readiness to use its armed forces as instruments of policy and power. It is an active participant in the new cold war and the arms race. The fact that it did not start the arms race is secondary to the fact of the massive nuclear overkill which it, like the USA, now mounts. In the end, what will matter is not origins, but outcomes. Soviet militarism is one part of the process which, unchecked, can lead us into the nuclear holocaust.

3. The foundations of militarism

Starting from the basic interests, worldviews and assumptions of the leaderships of the major states, it is possible to see a rational requirement for high military spending and large armed forces. But that is not enough if we want to understand how those requirements are translated into decisions which shape both budgets and forces. To do this, it is necessary to look at the organisations which form the social foundations of military spending.

These organisations have a decisive influence on the way in which requirements are met and, increasingly, on the way in which they are set. They develop an institutional rationality derived from their own sectional interests. They tend to be directed towards meeting short- and medium-term goals, and to be less interested in long-term outcomes. While these organisations and their political supporters will always claim to be advancing the interests of the state, their interpretation of state interest is refracted through their own rationalities. The result is an imperfect blend of various interests so that the state's requirements can appear to be met inadequately and irrationally.

In this chapter we discuss the role of these organisations in the advanced capitalist countries.

The military and bureaucracy

Roles and organisation
Modern armed forces are organised around their major weapons systems – integrated packages of weapons platform (ship, aircraft, tank, etc.), armament (guns, missiles,

etc.) and a means of communication. The central role of the weapon system began with the systematic application of large-scale technology to military purposes. Although they were not described in this way at the time, the large battleships built in the British–German naval arms race before the First World War were the first such weapon systems.[1]

Today, military personnel have become the necessary appendages of technological artefacts, human instruments of the weapon system. In each service, the major weapons systems form the apex of organisational hierarchies: aircraft carriers or other major surface vessels in the navy; bombers and fighters in the air force; tanks in the army. They are the core of the order of battle, the organising principle.

One consequence of this is that military confrontation and competition has come to be seen as a process of technological rivalry. It thus becomes axiomatic that every new step in the competition must involve increasing technological sophistication. But this extra sophistication comes neither cheaply nor quickly. The development of weapons systems from the drawing board to actual deployment can last a decade or more, involving tens of thousands of people and large investments through major corporations. Weapons entering service now were first designed ten years ago; weapons being designed now will not be operational until ten years hence. The result is a rolling programme of development and production, which both sustains an internal momentum to the arms race and creates inertia against fundamental changes in the nature or roles of military organisations.

The centrality of the weapon system thus rests on a marriage of technological sophistication and functional conservatism. In the armed forces, this only strengthens existing institutional inertia. As one writer has put it:

Exceptionally closed systems of this type are bound to have a congruence between qualifications, ideas and organisation. A candidate is not selected unless he fits the system fairly well. He is then indoctrinated in order to fit it better, whereupon he becomes a party to shaping the system by promoting his own kind from within and selecting them from without . . . Thus, in periods of prolonged peace, armed forces tend to remain self designed.[2]

Two characteristics of armed forces are crucial in this process of self-design – discipline and tradition. Strict discipline can be understood as a functional necessity for getting large numbers of people to risk their lives and function as a single unit. But it is not at all clear that the minutiae of rank and the rituals which surround them are a functional necessity in this same sense. What is clear is that most armed forces insist on them, fill the lives of service personnel with them and make them central in their self-image. The emphasis on tradition and experience is related to the emphasis on hierarchy and ritual. Tradition further promotes a collective self-image, providing a collective past with which individuals can identify.

It would not be accurate, however, to think of modern armed forces as utterly inflexible and impervious to change. In particular, warfare provides a harsh testing ground for old preferences and ways of doing things. If those which prove ineffectual are not discarded, the outcome is defeat or a needlessly high price for victory. Warfare thus enforces adaptation and improvisation; things continue to be done 'by the book', but the book can get rewritten. The return of peace settles the victorious forces back into a pattern in which self-design proceeds on a somewhat changed basis. But because they are largely closed organisations, armed forces manage to develop highly selective ways of learning.[3]

Entering the First World War the major European armies believed in the effectiveness of the offensive. This belief derived from the Napoleonic wars a century before and the Prussian wars against Austria and France in 1866 and 1870. It ethnocentrically ignored the lesson of the American Civil War which showed, like countless other wars, the costliness and futility of frontal assaults on strongly defended positions. On the western front, strategic conditions and relatively recent technology, whose tactical implications had been imperfectly assimilated, turned major offensives into blood-baths. Hundreds of thousands of lives were lost in periodic attempts to prove that trenches, barbed wire, deep mud and machine guns had not made offensives impracticable. After the war, the French army had learned about the strength of the defence. But the German army had learned about the potential of tanks and mobile warfare, and it drove an armoured offensive into France in 1940, skirting the Maginot Line. The tank was thus elevated to prime position and all modern armies have since organised themselves around it. In 1973, Egyptian infantry equipped with light and very accurate anti-tank missiles made a mess of Israeli armoured forces, promoting a continuing debate about the utility of tanks. So far this has not really dented the orthodoxy.

This history of selective learning could be retold for each of the services. The difficulties of learning produce odd twists in the procurement of major weapons systems.

During the Korean war, American pilots began to ask for relatively simple, light and highly manoeuvrable fighter aircraft. Studies around this theme resulted in an official requirement for such aircraft, and the Lockheed corporation won the contract. The aircraft it developed was the F-104, but by the mid-1950s the us Air Force was beginning to lose interest in the project. The lobby for the lightweight fighter was made up of people who had only recently been doing the fighting; they thus lacked the necessary seniority, and, once the war was over, their demands were of less importance. Few F-104s were purchased by the USA. Turned into a multi-role aircraft, however, the F-104 was successfully sold to several western European countries and Japan, with the aid of some corruption. Officially, the F-104 was dubbed the Starfighter; unofficially, in the West German air force it became known as the Widowmaker. Its propensity to crash on take-off may have had something to do with the way in which its weight was doubled when it was turned from a fighter into a multi-role aircraft.[4]

A similar story has occurred more recently. During the Vietnam war, American pilots were once again calling for a lightweight fighter. This contract was won by General Dynamics who developed the F-16. For sale to western European countries it too has become a multi-role aircraft, although this time the weight has been increased by a mere 50 per cent.[5] The aircraft which lost out when the US Air Force contract went to the F-16 was Northrop's F-18. This is now being purchased by the US navy and, having similarly started out as a cheap, simple, lightweight fighter, has ended up as an expensive, complex, heavy multi-role aircraft.

In this respect, weapons systems are like people: they are selected because they fit the system, and then shaped to fit it better. The very fact that the F-104, F-16 and F-18 all started out as lightweight fighters indicates that within the system there are individuals and groups who try to swim against the current and manage to have some influence. There is now a strong and increasingly vocal body of opinion within the US military which is heavily critical of the over-complex weapons systems which are now being designed and produced at such great expense.[6] But the evidence of the F-16, the F-18 and other projects such as the M-1 Abrams tank which, in familiar fashion, started out as cheap and simple and has ended up as the most elaborate and expensive tank ever built,[7] is that there is a powerful inertia in favour of continuing complexity.

In a more paradoxical form, this inertia is also felt in nuclear strategy. There is abundant evidence that the US military has never become fully accustomed to the idea of deterrence theory which says that the idea of having nuclear weapons is not to use them. Consistently, US armed services have sought strategies and technologies which place the emphasis less on the pure function of deterrence and more on the potential for fighting and winning a nuclear war. In the 1970s, backed by new generations of civilian strategists, and with nuclear weapons technologies becoming more sophisticated (and, especially, more accurate), they have increasingly had their way. Theories of 'limited nuclear war' fit better with the inherited self-image of the military than pure deterrence theories.[8]

Modern armed forces do make great efforts to understand changes in technology and their effects on tactics and strategy. In fact, it is possible to argue that they have come to pay too much attention to the ins and outs of new technological development. But while they are capable of learning, they are most capable of learning lessons which confirm and extend existing prejudices. The insistence on ever-greater sophistication in major weapon systems has resulted in extremely expensive products which are constantly going wrong and require a great deal of maintenance. This does not seem to be the best way of meeting the state's requirement for armed force, but the evidence of the period since 1945 suggests that it may be the only way that modern armed forces know.

Bureaucratic politics

So far we have been referring to 'the military'. But military spending also provides directly for the employment of many thousands of civilians. Table 3.1 shows the figures for Britain. As a large organisation deploying considerable resources and fulfilling crucial state requirements, the military establishment, including its civilian bureaucracy, has tremendous influence with which to protect and promote its sectional interests. But within the military, interests diverge between the different groups.

Among the critics of orthodox theories of military spending are those who stress these factors and advance theories of bureaucratic politics to explain how military spending is determined.[9] By pointing to the weight of the military bureaucracies and their allies, and to the manoeuvring for position and power games that they indulge in, these theories do a real service to those seeking to understand military and strategic decision-making. But it is also important to recognise the limits of the power of the

Table 3.1 UK **military employment 1981 (thousands)**

Royal Navy	66·4	
Royal Marines	7·9	
Army	166·0	
RAF	93·5	
Total regular forces		334
UK civilian staff		
Non-industrial	103·1	
Industrial	120·6	
Total		224*
Defence contractors†		
Direct employment on MOD contracts	310	
Indirect employment on MOD contracts	270	
Employment for arms exports	140	
Total		720
Overall total		1,278

Notes:
*   Royal Ordnance Factories accounted for 21 of this total. The total does not include 41 employed abroad.
†   All estimates of defence industry employment have a large margin of error. These official figures seem likely to be overestimates.
Source: 'Statement on the Defence Estimates 1982', HMSO, Cmnd 8529.

bureaucracies. A recent useful example in Britain was the effort of the Ministry of Defence to avoid being subjected to the 'cash limit' controls on public spending which are part of government policy. Despite the Conservative government's predisposition to support a powerful and free-spending military, the Ministry of Defence finally lost the battle, if not the war. Even the most powerful of bureaucracies can be overridden. It is also necessary to bear in mind that theories of bureaucratic politics as a driving force in building up armaments make an important contribution to explaining the process, but have little to say about its origins. The power of the bureaucracy derives from the state's political requirements. However, as time passes, the bureaucracy, as a part of the state apparatus, becomes influential in setting those requirements.

A critical instrument in this process is control of information. Senior officers and civil servants function as sources of expert advice to the government of the day because of their privileged access to information. Government policy is shaped by this bureaucratic control of information. The information is either withheld from, or selectively fed into, the public domain in a way which will persuade public opinion to support official policy. Much of what is kept secret would be of no assistance whatsoever to the USSR which probably knows it already, but it might well weaken the power, credibility and mystique of the bureaucracy.

What is most useful about secrecy is that it reduces accountability for actions undertaken, and especially for failures and incompetence. As a result, it goes well beyond what can be justified by genuine security concerns and becomes, ultimately, a deeply engrained habit, and even a need. As Dixon has put it:

> By divulging information a professional in-group may feel that it is losing some of its mystique, thereby weakening its image in the eyes of the public, and this loss will be the greatest precisely when the in-group is most at a loss as to what to do next.[10]

From its privileged position as the repository of knowledge and expertise, a military bureaucracy will always try to avoid offering policy advice which would act against its sectional interest. Asked if military spending should be increased, it is hard to imagine the bureaucracy saying 'no'. In general, military bureaucracies seek as much as they can get, and then complain that what they have is insufficient, so that they can sustain their case for increased spending next time round. A military bureaucracy is thus a permanent source of pressure for higher military spending. How successful it is will depend on the government's political and economic orientation, the pressures for higher spending by other government departments and the general economic and political circumstances.

United in seeking the biggest possible budget, the bureaucracy tends to be more divided in other matters, especially on the allocation of resources within the budget when finances are tight. In the lead-up to the British decision in 1980 to purchase Trident strategic nuclear missiles and submarines for the navy, it became clear that the other two services were anxious lest their own programmes be cut to make room for Trident. In the 1981 defence review, the army and air force were successful in ensuring that the navy bore the brunt of the cuts which the Trident decision necessitated. In the wake of war in the south Atlantic, however, it seems possible that those naval cuts will be rescinded. Unless military spending can be further increased, the army and air force will have another fight on their hands.

A different kind of bureaucratic battle is exemplified by the fight in the USA in the 1950s between army and air force over who should have responsibility for intermediate-range nuclear missiles. When the Thor missile was adopted, this meant an air force victory; the army had been pushing for the Jupiter missile. It was also a victory for the air force's ally, the aerospace industry; Jupiter would have been manufactured by Chrysler, which also makes tanks.[11] In the planned deployment of Pershing II missiles to West Germany in the 1980s, part of the story is the US Army re-fighting that old battle, this time successfully. With Pershing II it will at last be equipped with a nuclear weapon which can be targeted against the USSR, finally winning a niche along with the navy and air force in the strategic nuclear mission.[12]

These divisions between the services are cross-cut by divisions between the uniformed and civilian components of the military establishment, especially around issues of administrative control. Each service tends to prefer the greatest possible institutional autonomy, but this tends to conflict with centralised planning of the military effort as a whole, which is usually the task of civilians along with the most senior uniformed officers. In the 1960s, seeking to co-ordinate planning more tightly (against pressure from the services) Robert McNamara, the US Defense Secretary, established the Office of Systems Analysis, staffed by civilians, to develop a centralised source of expertise on key strategic questions to counterbalance the analyses produced by the services.[13] His success was only limited. An insider's account makes it clear that in the field of cost controls, civilians and uniformed officers alike connived to administer vast waste and disguise it from the US Congress.[14]

Out of these cross-cutting divisions, bureaucratic politics consist of constantly shifting alliances and coalitions. The services, administrators, scientists and economists pit themselves against each other in ever-changing combinations. Arms corporations seeking major contracts, and politicians supporting local interests, intervene to spice up the process further. From these Byzantine court intrigues come the detailed decisions on allocating available military resources, as issues of vast import are settled through the balance of petty interest and bureaucratic habits.

Industry and technology

As a rough rule of thumb, one can usually expect about 35 per cent of a state's annual military spending to be devoted to equipment. Pay for military and civilian staff usually takes a rather larger proportion, with the remainder spent on buildings, stores and various miscellaneous items.

Britain has spent a greater than average proportion of its annual military budget on equipment and this proportion has been rising in recent years. This reflects the capital-intensive nature of British military spending, and reveals the tendency for spending on equipment to squeeze spending on personnel.

The aerospace industry is the major industrial beneficiary of military spending. Next in the list is the electronics industry; much of its production is also for aerospace projects. The aerospace industry was for a time largely state-owned, and Ministry of Defence contracts account for about half its total output. Shipbuilding is wholly state-owned, and Ministry of Defence contracts account for about one-third of its output. About a third of the privately owned electronics industry's output is for such contracts.

In 1981–82 the equipment budget totalled about £5,850 million. About 90 per cent of this went to British companies, the rest abroad for equipment imports. Of the seven companies receiving more than £100 million, only Plessey (electronics) and Westland (helicopters) were privately owned. The Ministry of Defence estimates that it has contracts with 10,000 companies which provide jobs for about 580,000 people in Britain, half of them working in companies which specialise in military production.[15] About one million people in Britain work in jobs which depend on military spending. An estimated further 140,000 jobs are provided by arms exports, so about 720,000 industrial jobs depend on arms, and about 1.3 million overall. The value of these arms exports for 1981–82 was estimated at £1,500 million, which means that the total value of arms production in Britain (i.e. excluding military imports) was of the order of £6,800 million – about 3 per cent of GDP.

The major corporations

The immediate beneficiaries of arms contracts are the corporations which develop and produce the equipment. The extent to which they depend on military contracts varies widely. Table 3.2 lists the top 20 western European contractors. The electronics companies tend to be far less dependent on military work than the others; among aerospace companies, the British and French depend more heavily on military work than the West German ones. In the USA, it is reported that by 1975 the top 25 arms producers' military work accounted for less than 10 per cent of their total turnover (compared to 40 per cent in 1958). But the degree of variation is revealed by the fact that 75 per cent of new ship construction in the USA is for the US Navy.[16] Arms producers that have diversified their operations have tended to do this by acquiring other companies, leaving their military divisions highly specialised and highly dependent on military contracts.

Table 3.2 **Western Europe's top 20 arms producers, 1977**

Company	Country	Arms production turnover, 1977 (£m)	Percentage of arms production in total turnover 1977
1 Thomson	France	750	33
2 SNIAS	France	740	75
3 British Aerospace	UK	625	80
4 Dassault	France	600	91
5 DTCN	France	575	100
6 Siemens	West Germany	500	8
7 Rolls-Royce	UK	475	70
8 Oerlikon-Buerhle	Switzerland	400	60
9 GIAT	France	370	100
10 AEG	West Germany	350	10
11 GEC	UK	340	15
12 MBB	West Germany	270	60
13 VFW-Fokker	West Germany	255	60
14 Philips	Netherlands	250	3
15 SNECMA	France	250	65
16 Krauss-Maffei	West Germany	175	70
17 Vickers	UK	155	40
18 Royal Ordnance Factories	UK	145	100
19 Bofors	Sweden	145	55
20 Fincantieri	Italy	140	33

Source: Armaments and Underdevelopment Working Group, Institute for Peace Research and Security Policy, University of Hamburg.

This dependence, however, is a complex matter. Certain states see military–industrial capacity as crucial to their security. They therefore have to nourish the industry, providing it with regular work, sustaining innovation. The dependence thus works both ways.

Some critics of the military–industrial complex have tended to oversimplify this relationship when arguing that it is the corporate requirements of the arms producers which determine weapons procurement, strategy and military spending. Partly, this results from over-concentration on the

USA where the large corporations often function as laws unto themselves and carry a good deal of political clout. There is a clear record of US admirals and generals retiring from the military and entering senior executive positions with companies from which they used to order arms. But the image of a shadowy conspiracy based in the corporations running the show with help from well-placed members of the state bureaucracy is not always helpful for understanding what goes on.

In Britain and France, the state has reorganised the arms industries over the years, nationalising large chunks of them. In the USA, the state baled out Lockheed when it got into trouble in the early 1970s, but would not do the same for Grumman when it overspent on the development of the extremely sophisticated F-14 fighter aircraft. It was the Shah of Iran who saved Grumman, largely because he was infatuated by the F-14.[17] Further, the arms industry is not just made up of the giant corporations. It also consists of thousands of small and medium-sized companies, whose numbers in the USA declined from over 6,000 to under 4,000 between 1968 and 1975.[18]

The military–industrial complex, in general, functions not on the basis of conspiracy (though that happens) nor on the basis of bribery and corruption (though they also happen, especially if one recognises that not all bribery is legally corrupt). Rather, it functions on the basis of a structural pairing that inevitably develops into mutual interests.

Both the military and the corporations require high military spending. Both are organised around major items of equipment, for use and for production. Corporations tend to specialise in particular equipment for particular parts of the armed forces. Close ties develop in the process of specifying, modifying, working on and checking the requirements for equipment. It is in these ties between particular corporations and particular parts of the military (rather than between military industry as a whole and the military as a whole) that the military–industrial complex has been constructed. It is also in these ties that the opportunities, and the temptations, arise for straying into conspiracy, bribery and corruption. But in the context of technologically sophisticated armed forces, weapons procurement could barely work at all without such ties developing.

This symbiosis is based on two fundamental politico-strategic assumptions, which it then reinforces. The first is the assumption that national self-sufficiency in arms production is a requirement of state policy and security. The second is the assumption that advanced and advancing technology is also a security requirement. The structural pairing of armed forces and arms industries is the first inevitable result of these assumptions. The second result is that the major suppliers become influential in determining how the military budget is spent and in setting the gross level of expenditure. This influence works both directly, through contacts with the military and bureaucracy, and indirectly through the political arena.

Naturally, this corporate influence is exerted to keep military spending high and raise it where possible. In this, the arms corporations are united. But, as with the military bureaucracies, there are elements of competition in determining how the budget is spent. It is not the same kind of competition as between, say, different manufacturers of cars or headache-cures, and it is rarely competition about price. Military industry does not function in a 'free' market, because the 'market' consists of a single purchaser, the state, which also acts as an export agent for the producers and has the power to prevent exports. In the USA, various attempts have been made to introduce 'free' market relations into arms production and procurement by having two corporations develop weaponry in competition with each other. These attempts have usually failed in the face of opposing pressures. Thus, the F-18 was originally the 'loser' in the competition for the US air force contract won by the F-16, but the F-18 was later taken up by the US navy.

The competition between arms corporations consists of the efforts by each to maintain its share of a 'market' limited by the size of the military budget. If one corporation gets a contract for a new bomber, another corporation loses out. But a third corporation, producing fighters, and even a fourth, producing submarines or tanks, may also lose out if the contract for the new bomber consumes budgetary resources which might otherwise have come their way. Thus, even where there is only one airframe and one aero-engine company, as in Britain, they are still involved in a competition with other arms producers in different industrial sectors. This level of competition parallels and intensifies the intrigues and manoeuvring within the military bureaucracies, bringing further interests into play in the implementation of state security policy.

Technological momentum

Many people believe that military technology has a momentum all its own, devoid of rational justification or control. Close examination of the more exotic military technology provides much evidence to confirm this view. The key to this momentum, which is a product of human choice, not natural law, lies in the balance of interdependence between the state and the military industry.

The military will always want improved equipment. This is only human. They will jump at improvements offered to them and seek to identify possible improvements through 'in-house' research. The arms corporations have little use for a one-off military contract. They need to guarantee production for years ahead, seek constantly for new development contracts to replace existing ones, and therefore also conduct independent research on possible technological improvements.

With both the military and the major corporations looking ahead, the result is often that 'solutions' emerge before anybody has identified the 'problems' they can solve. In the US Pentagon, the Advanced Research Projects Agency spends large amounts of time and money identifying bizarre solutions to problems which are equally bizarre or unidentified. The idea of laser weapons was around for many years before anybody figured out how they could be used.[19] The basic design of the neutron bomb originated during the late 1950s (and the idea of it emerged during the original Second World War atom bomb project); it was first offered as a solution to the problems of tactical nuclear warfare, then for the problems of shooting down strategic missiles, before it was finally agreed that its appropriate problem was actually tactical nuclear warfare.[20]

This whole process is underpinned not only by the requirements of the industry, but also by a definite philosophy of technology which can be summarised in three parts: all problems have technological solutions; the best solution is the most complex one; if it *can* be done, it *ought* to be done. Even where the problem is identified before the solution is found, the emphasis is always on new improvements in the products. New weapon projects can be justified only if they are better than their predecessors, and it is rare for 'better' to mean 'cheaper' or 'simpler'.

The result is a rolling programme of development and production. The difficulty here is that, from the perspective of an arms corporation, the ideal operational 'life' of a weapon system should correspond to the manufacturing cycle, so that new weapons will be phased in to fill the gaps as old weapons are phased out. So the operational 'life' of weapons systems must be reduced by showing how they have become obsolescent, by showing that even if they still work reasonably well they are inferior to what the Russians have got, or to what the military could have, or both.

Technological development along limited performance dimensions (providing greater speed, accuracy, protection, manoeuvrability, endurance, and so on) leads into a cul-de-sac. In time, further improvements become impossible or hugely expensive. They may well fail to improve actual combat capability, or may even *reduce* that capability.[21] Major improvements in capability are provided only by rare technological breakthroughs, and are usually associated with a redefinition of roles and missions. As technologies mature, marginal improvements in performance become less important, more expensive and dependent on greater complexity. This means fewer items of equipment can be bought, while their complexity makes them harder to maintain and more prone to breaking down. In a sense, technologies go beyond maturity, become overripe and decay.

A state which is committed to maintaining military–industrial capacity can do little about this process once it has become rooted in industry and the military. To be kept in being, military–industrial capacity must be kept in work. This especially means that development capacity must be kept working on new ideas, new improvements. But new improvements are more demanding, and development capacity must therefore expand, and then justify itself anew with more improvements, leading to further expansion. Momentum generates momentum. Without countervailing measures, development capacity could expand indefinitely.

The countervailing policies available to the state in the main arms-producing countries can focus on the size or the cost of development capacity. Its expansion can be limited by increasing the time each development project takes, by not proceeding from development to production, or by reorganising the industry to eliminate duplication of effort. Costs can be limited by internationalising them, either by boosting arms exports or by participating in collaborative international projects. So far, none of these policies has actually restrained the momentum of military technology.

The arms trade

Data on the international arms trade are, if anything, even more suspect than data on military spending. However, the two main sources of data, the US Arms Control and Disarmament Agency and the Stockholm International Peace Research Institute, agree that the value of the trade at least doubled during the 1970s. Less developed countries, especially in the Middle East, increased their imports particularly sharply. More states joined the ranks of arms exporters in the 1970s, and the western European exporters increased their share of the market.[22]

The boom in the trade reflects increased demand for sophisticated weaponry. But, as in any market, demand is not entirely autonomous. The main exporting states have established large specialised agencies to promote exports, backed by regular exhibitions of their latest wares; and there is an extensive and notorious record of unscrupulous and corrupt selling practices.[23]

In those states for which maintaining military industry is a part of security policy, arms exports have also become a part of the policy. Without exports, either the arms corporations would have to contract, or the military budget would have to increase to provide extra demand. Efforts to agree restraints on arms exports have therefore got nowhere. Yet it is hard to believe that a recklessly expanding arms trade is good for global security or, therefore, for the security of the exporting states. When Britain went to war with Argentina, it faced this contradiction directly: Argentina was equipped with weapons exported to it by Britain's allies and by Britain itself.

Exporters and importers alike are locked into a system in which each feeds off the other. Imports sustain burgeoning military and bureaucratic institutions which require further imports to reproduce themselves. Exports not only sustain but even expand production capacity which requires yet more exports to continue operating. At the same time as this sharpens the competition in an expanding market, many of the importing states have begun to develop indigenous arms production capacity and some have begun to export weapons on their own account. This generates a ceaseless search for new markets. Many corporations' eyes are now greedily turned on China, hoping both that it will opt for high technology weapons and that advanced capitalist states will steadily overcome their inhibitions about selling arms to communists.

International collaboration
The boom in the arms trade has been accompanied by an increasing internationalisation of arms production. In early

1982 there were about 200 weapons projects planned and under way worldwide in which two or more states were participating in designing or producing major weapons together.[24] This network of deals on collaborative design, co-production, licensed production or assembly, involves both industrialised and less developed countries.

The less developed countries tend to produce weaponry designed in an industrialised country. The aim is to cut the foreign exchange costs of procuring new equipment and to end exclusive dependence on imports. But the process has contradictory results. Aspects of the technology involved in producing sophisticated weapons are transferred to the poorer country, but control over the technology is not. So it is necessary to enter further deals for further production licences in order to sustain the new production capacity. Furthermore, because development and production techniques among the industrialised states are not uniform, it may be necessary to return time and again to the same state. Thus, a less developed country which begins to produce arms may simply re-emphasise its dependence on the exporters by a new route.

The key to gaining control of technology is in creating a fully fledged development capacity which can reproduce and adapt the technology. But this is not only a highly expensive and lengthy process; it is also very difficult. The most successful example of it in the arms field is probably Westland, the British helicopter company, which built its expertise partly through successive production licences from the USA in the 1950s and 1960s. It has now broken away from US industry, developed its own helicopters and shared in development projects with France, Italy and West Germany. To some extent, Israel has also managed to do it with fighter aircraft, but remains handicapped by weaknesses in aero-engine technology. So far, other less developed countries have found it extremely difficult to follow suit.

Collaboration in developing and producing major weapons has become an important feature of arms production in NATO. Up to 1967 about 8 per cent of procurement projects (except naval procurement, where the figure was much lower) involved any kind of collaboration. Mostly, this was a matter of western European states producing US-designed equipment. In the following decade, the proportion rose to 20 per cent, of which just under half involved the USA. The trend towards collaboration was sharpest in aerospace to begin with, but is strong now in missiles and armoured vehicles as well.[25]

For projects in which western European states have merely produced equipment designed by the USA, the motivation and the problems are similar to those in the case of less developed countries beginning arms production. But several major projects now involve collaboration between western European states right from the outset, in the early design stage. Here the motivation stems from the momentum of military technology and the need to restrain the costs of development capacity. In essence, arms industries are beginning to outgrow the national arena. A single western European state cannot afford to develop independently the full range of the most sophisticated new equipment. If the armed forces will not accept second best, if exports are not regarded as a sufficiently firm guarantee of a long production run which might reduce unit costs, and if reliance on the USA is unacceptable, the only option is to attempt to share the costs of development with other states in a similar position.

There are several problems in collaborative development. The first is the series of battles that begin immediately about which countries and which corporations get the plum development contracts. The second is that collaboration tends to increase the time taken for development. The third is that procurement schedules in different states are not always compatible. The fourth is that the different western European armed forces have developed different doctrines for the use of similar kinds of equipment and tend to have different operational requirements. The effort to reconcile conflicting requirements and preferences in a single weapon system increases its complexity and its cost, making it more sophisticated than any one of the collaborating states wants it to be. As a result, the apparent cost-savings of collaboration may be illusory, and collaboration becomes yet another mechanism driving on technological momentum. The major collaborative project in western Europe is the British–German–Italian Tornado multi-role aircraft; German critics long since labelled it 'the egg-laying, wool-producing, milk-giving sow'.[26] Such strange beasts are not cheap.

There is a final paradox to collaboration. States enter it to sustain an industrial capability which they have decided is important for their security. They would not believe that capability mattered for their security if they did not link their concept of security to national sovereignty. Yet by collaborating in developing major weapons, national sovereignty is compromised because the military–industrial capability ceases to be quite so autonomous.

Ambitious plans to unify the procurement policies of the western European states and develop multinational arms corporations bring out the logic of collaboration and extend it. They seek to create a single supra-national agency to manage the development, production and procurement of major weapons.[27] Rivalries within western Europe have undermined the drive for such integration in recent years, and the USA remains central to western European military strategy. These two factors have prevented the implementation of such grandiose schemes. Whether they will find a place in the politics of the 1980s remains to be seen. But if they do, national parliaments and political forces operating within a purely national arena will find it even harder to control or influence crucial aspects of military policy and the size of the budget. If they do not, however, there will be increased pressure on national resources from the onward march of military technology. Neither option provides much comfort.

4. The economic consequences of military spending

It is often argued that military spending is economically necessary in that it generates jobs, technological advance, or growth which could not be provided by other means. If this were true, it would mean that disarmament would involve large economic costs. However, all the available evidence suggests that this argument is not true. Rather than benefiting the economy, military expenditure imposes a substantial burden. To demonstrate how this burden arises we will examine the economic consequences of military spending in some detail. To do this properly we have to be a little more technical and rely more heavily on economic terms than in the rest of the book. The reader who is willing to take the harmful effects of military expenditure on trust can rush straight on to disarmament in chapter 5.

Although we use a framework of economic theory in this chapter we cannot just rely on the standard economic categories and calculations which are usually applied to government spending. There are specific economic effects which are peculiar to military spending and which do not ensue from spending on, say, education, health or roads. These specific effects tend to be more important in the long run, therefore it is important to distinguish the immediate effects from the longer term impact of a change in military expenditure. For example, in the short run, an increase in the defence budget might raise output and employment but it would also influence investment, productivity growth, the balance of payments and private decisions on savings and consumption. The changes in these variables would then, after some delay, feed back to the system. As a result of these second-round effects, the initial rise in output and employment may be more than offset. The end result would then be lower, not higher, output and employment. Since the longer-term effects tend to influence rates of economic growth and to accumulate over time, it is important to track them down. Given the importance of the distinction between short-run and long-run effects, we look at the influence of military expenditure in two stages. In the first section, we examine the immediate impact using categories from orthodox economic analysis, while the second section uses marxist categories to examine the longer-term structural effects.

The argument that military expenditure is necessary to maintain jobs is so widespread, that it seems useful to consider the relationship with employment in more detail. This is done in the section entitled 'Unemployment'. Sometimes the argument that military expenditure is necessary or beneficial to the economy is extended to suggest that these economic consequences provide a major motive for military expenditure. We examine this functionalist explanation, that the state spends on defence for economic reasons, in the final section of this chapter, 'Economic Motivations of Military Spending'.

Immediate effects

One manifestation of the current economic crisis is the deep division among orthodox economists. Our argument here will be largely Keynesian because the theory is rather more coherent with respect to military spending than its alternatives. Monetarist theories emphasise the damaging effects of high government spending, but military spending gets exempted from the criticism on ideological grounds. This ambivalence is reflected in monetarist analyses.

The Keynesian argument begins with the proposition that raising military spending will raise aggregate demand, the total spending in the economy. What happens next depends on the relationship between aggregate demand and aggregate supply, the capacity to produce. We assume, for the moment, that the extra military spending is all spent within the country concerned.

Aggregate supply is the potential economic output that can be produced in a particular country. It is determined by the size of the available labour force, by the existing stock of capital (plant, machinery, etc.) and by the efficiency with which labour and capital are used. If this potential supply is greater than actual spending, an increase in military demand would increase output and thus reduce unemployment. Any increase in government spending would have the same effect.

The extent to which unemployment is reduced will depend on two things: what the extra money is spent on, and what kinds and numbers of people are unemployed. Increasing the number of people in the armed forces would initially create more jobs than spending the same money on buying more equipment from domestic industry. The second-round effects, which come from people newly employed spending their extra income, will depend on whether the additional military personnel are low-paid conscripts or professionals. If the extra spending is used to purchase equipment, the reduction in unemployment will be smaller the more capital-intensive arms production is, and larger the more that new arms production replaces imports. But the effect on unemployment may be limited if, even at a time of high measured unemployment, there is a shortage of workers with the particular skills required in the arms industry.

The size of these effects will also depend on how the extra military spending is financed. If taxes are raised to pay for it, the increases in output and employment will be smaller and will vary depending on whether the method used is direct (e.g. income tax) or indirect (e.g. VAT). If taxes are not increased, then the government deficit (or Public Sector Borrowing Requirement – the PSBR) will increase, and the effects will differ according to whether this is matched by increased borrowing or an increase in the supply of money.

The exact size of the increase in output and employment thus depends on a very large number of factors. But as long as there was spare capacity to begin with, and as long as taxes are not increased by more than is needed to finance the extra military spending, output and employment should both increase.

However, we should also ask why there was spare capacity to begin with: why was output less than it could have been? It seems more likely that this would result from constraints on the supply side than from inadequate demand alone. Unless increasing military spending removed these constraints, they would continue to operate after the increase and cause other adjustments in the system. So far we have been looking at what happens when supply increases to meet the extra demand created by higher military spending. But it is also necessary to look at what happens when supply cannot adjust. If supply does not meet the extra demand, there are four main ways in which the system could adjust. First, real military spending might not increase by the planned amount. Second, inflation could increase, causing other adjustments. Third, other spending may be displaced. Fourth, the balance of payments could deteriorate.

In Britain at the time of the Korean war, the Labour government planned a major programme of rearmament. Much of this went ahead, but the target of spending 12 per cent of the GDP on the military could not be fulfilled because of shortages of resources. The Conservative government which took over from Labour recognised these constraints and cut back the plans accordingly. At peak, 10·5 per cent of GDP was spent on the military. Similar supply constraints prevented targets being met when President Carter increased US military spending in 1980.[1] Excess demand can also result in higher inflation, so that the money allocated to the military actually buys less even if supply is available.

If the extra military demand is met, then the adjustments occur elsewhere in the system as other spending is crowded out, or displaced. This can happen in a variety of ways. It may be a direct displacement, as in the Korean war rearmament in Britain: products, labour, plant and machinery which had been dedicated largely to making capital goods for investment and export were switched to meeting military orders. Alternatively, the increased military demand may induce higher inflation which cuts real purchasing power, thus reducing private demand. The same thing results from raising taxes to finance the extra spending, and from raising interest rates to cover any increase in the government deficit. In each case, other forms of demand are displaced. Which component of aggregate demand bears the brunt is largely an empirical question.

Investment

The evidence is that it is investment or fixed capital formation – the purchase of plant and equipment for use in production – which is the major component of demand to be displaced by military spending. Among advanced capitalist countries, and on average across time within each country, there is almost an exact one-to-one relationship. An increase of 1 per cent in the share of output devoted to military spending is associated with a fall of 1 per cent in the share of output devoted to capital formation.[2]

There are two main reasons for this trade-off. The first is that the main arms industries – aerospace, shipbuilding, electronics and engineering – also produce investment goods. Their military output diverts resources from investment. The second reason is that, over the long term, total non-military consumption (i.e. purchases of goods and services) by government and by private individuals combine to form a relatively stable share of total demand relative to the rate of economic growth and the rate of unemployment. Increases in military spending do not generally shift this relationship. It is therefore investment which has to adjust.

The result of investment being displaced is that less is added to the capital stock and the rate of growth of productivity is lower. In turn, this reduces the rate of economic growth. Future levels of economic output are lower than they would otherwise have been. This effect is visible in the data in Tables 4.1 and 4.2 which show the

Table 4.1 Military spending and the economy, 1954–73

	Average shares (%) of output devoted to:		Average rates (%) of:	
	Investment	Military spending	Growth	Unemployment
Australia	24·8	3·1	4·9	1·2
Austria	27·9	1·3	5·4	3·3
Belgium	19·9	3·2	4·2	3·8
Canada	26·3	4·3	5·0	5·3
Denmark	20·2	2·7	4·4	5·0
France	22·5	5·5	5·6	1·3
West Germany	24·4	3·8	6·1	1·0
Italy	22·3	3·6	5·3	4·7
Japan	33·4	1·1	10·1	1·2
Netherlands	24·6	4·1	5·1	1·3
Sweden	22·8	4·1	3·7	1·7
Switzerland	26·5	2·6	4·2	0·15
UK	16·6	6·1	2·9	2·7
USA	16·4	8·3	3·9	5·0

Sources: OECD, *National Accounts Statistics* and *Economic Outlook*, various years; *World Armaments and Disarmament: SIPRI Yearbook*, various years.

average shares of output devoted to investment and military spending in the advanced capitalist countries, together with average rates of growth and unemployment. The two countries allocating the largest shares of output to the military were the USA and the UK. They also experienced the lowest rates of growth during the long boom. Military spending by advanced capitalist states undermines the economic strength of the society it is supposed to protect.

Balance of payments

Military spending can affect a country's balance of payments in a number of ways. If raising military spending increases demand beyond what can be met by industries producing for domestic consumption, either goods are diverted from being exported or imports flow in, or both. As a result, the balance of payments deteriorates. Depending on the effects of this on inflation and the state's monetary

Table 4.2 **Military spending and the economy, 1977**

| | Share (%) of output devoted to: | | Rate (%) of: | |
	Investment	*Military spending*	*Growth (average 1974–78)*	*Unemployment*
Australia	22·7	2·6	2·4	5·6
Austria	29·3	1·2	2·4	1·6
Belgium	21·5	3·2	1·8	7·5
Canada	22·8	1·9	3·2	8·0
Denmark	23·5	2·3	2·3	not available
France	23·5	3·9	2·9	4·7
West Germany	21·8	3·4	2·3	4·5
Italy	21·1	2·4	1·6	6·0
Japan	30·7	0·9	4·8	2·0
Netherlands	22·6	3·5	2·3	4·2
Sweden	19·7	3·4	0·5	1·8
Switzerland	20·8	2·1	−1·6	not available
UK	19·1	4·8	1·8	6·1
USA	18·5	5·4	3·5	7·1

Sources: OECD, *National Accounts Statistics* and *Economic Outlook*, various years; *World Armaments and Disarmament: SIPRI Yearbook*, various years.

and fiscal policies, this may induce changes in the exchange rate which then feed back to the system. A weak balance of payments may put pressure on the government to 'deflate' the economy by reducing demand, resulting in a lower economic growth rate.

But there are also specifically military trade flows. To analyse their patterns it is necessary to distinguish between 'visible' and 'invisible' trade on the military account. Visibles are goods (arms and other equipment) while invisibles are services (foreign military aid, advisors, expenditure and income associated with foreign bases).

The general pattern is for a country with a low absolute level of military spending to have a small arms industry. The state must import most of the equipment it requires and therefore has a deficit on visible trade on the military account. If its military spending increases over time, the arms industry may also grow, producing equipment which was previously imported and exporting as well. As a result, the visible balance would move into surplus. An example of this is West Germany since it began serious rearmament in the 1950s: its visible balance on the military account went into surplus in 1976.[3]

On the other hand, states with low military spending often receive military aid from a larger power. If military spending increases, and especially if forces begin to be stationed abroad, this aid would probably cease and the costs of foreign bases would have to be met. As a result, the invisible balance would move into deficit.

Thus high military spending tends to be associated with a visible surplus and an invisible deficit on the military account. The net effect on the overall balance of payments depends on the balance between these two parts of the military account. Some states such as France, Japan and West Germany have geared their policies to ensure a favourable balance. But for the USA and the UK it has been unfavourable. One estimate for 1950 to 1970 shows a net US deficit on the military account of $53 billion for the whole period, while for Britain it was about $7 billion.[4] However, this pattern may now be changing. In the USA, sales have replaced grants as the way of transferring military equipment to other states; in the 1950s over 90 per cent of transfers were aid, but by the end of the 1970s government sales accounted for over 90 per cent of transfers, with the remainder being sales by private companies.[5] In the UK, although the data are incomplete, it seems that by the end of the 1970s the large surplus on visibles and deficit on invisibles were roughly in balance with each other.[6]

Longer-term effects

Exchange

The sphere of exchange, or circulation, is the part of the accumulation process in which commodities, having been produced, are bought and sold. Some marxists have argued that a major contradiction within exchange, referred to as the 'realisation' problem, lies at the heart of capitalist crises.[7] They argue that it is in the nature of capitalism that potential production tends to outstrip potential demand because the growth of the latter is held back by capitalist pressures to keep wages down. But if demand does not grow adequately, capitalists will be unable to *realise* their profits because their products will not all be sold. This tendency to produce more than can be consumed pushes the system into stagnation and mass unemployment unless the state takes remedial action. This is often referred to as the 'under-consumptionist' theory of crisis.

According to the theory, the structure of power in capitalist societies limits the possibilities for remedial action by the state. It cannot take action which would undermine profits. Military spending is seen as the major way in which demand can be expanded to absorb excess production. Unlike some other types of government spending it is ideologically suitable. It does not threaten profits or capitalist control of production. By this account, high military spending was a major factor in creating low unemployment during the long economic boom to 1973.

Underconsumptionist explanations of military spending were most popular before the onset of the economic crises and recessions of the 1970s. Their main attraction appears to lie in a simple contrast: before the Second World War employment and military spending were both lower than they were during the long boom to 1973. The theory links the two with a causal explanation. But it is both theoretically and empirically inadequate.[8] Tables 4.1 and 4.2 show there is no association between average rates of unemployment and shares of output allocated to military spending. This is confirmed by analysis of each country. The random pattern suggests there is no general mechanism by which the proportion of output spent on the military influences the rate of unemployment. Moreover, there is no evidence that states have systematically used military spending since the Second World War as a way of reducing unemployment or resisting the tendency towards economic stagnation. Capitalist states have a wide range of policy instruments for regulating the economy, and the rate of unemployment seems to have been determined independently of the requirement for military spending.

Before the crises of the 1970s military spending did contribute to general economic growth, but not in the way that underconsumptionism suggests. The success of international regulation under US hegemony was a major factor in providing the conditions for the long boom. This leading role was underwritten to an important extent by US military power, and therefore by US military spending. The contribution of military spending to maintaining effective demand was thus indirect, and largely specific to US military spending. But high military spending eventually undermined the US economy, partly through its effects via investment and productivity on the growth rate, and partly through the weakening of the dollar as a result of the USA's global military role and the war in Vietnam. In the sphere of exchange, the results are now felt as a catastrophic slump in world trade. Having contributed for many years to the maintenance of stable conditions for exchange, military spending contradictorily contributed to the erosion of that stability.

Distribution

Distribution concerns the division of output into wages and profits. The share that goes to each depends on several factors: on conditions in the sphere of exchange such as the extent to which industrial capacity is utilised and the rate of unemployment; on conditions in the sphere of production, such as the discipline of the labour force and the degree of control by management of the work process; on the nature of state intervention in the economy, such as the structure of taxation and the maintenance of a 'social wage' in the form of free education and health services and social security; and on the balance of class forces – the relative political and ideological unity and strength of labour and capital. The distribution of power is thus a critical issue in the distribution of wealth.

Militarism has a variety of effects within power relations in capitalist societies. Military spending both sustains and is sustained by an ideology based on perceptions of threat to the established order and the need to respond to it. Promoting military values may help develop feelings of national unity, prestige and discipline, making workers more amenable to accepting the social order and their place within it. Conscription may take this further, especially by integrating disparate social and ethnic groups into the social whole. The ideology of the cold war can be used to isolate the most militant workers and trade-unionists, to divide political opposition and to legitimise harassment of it.

Beyond this, military power is the final guarantor of the state's power in domestic society. In normal circumstances, this function is unseen and unfelt by most people. But when labour discipline and national consensus break down, the military are available to break strikes, maintain essential services or repress public disorder. A violent head-on challenge to the state's authority would be met in similar terms by the state, which can call on its armed forces as well as the police. If the state's regulation of social relations is in danger of breaking down, it is ultimately the military on which the maintenance of the existing distribution of power and wealth would depend.

Production

Through military spending and the purchases of equipment which it generates, the state has a direct influence in the process of production. Much military research and development is directly financed by the state, providing it with the ability to influence the technological direction of the arms industry whether the corporations are privately or publicly owned. Western European states have used the influence accruing from military contracts to reorganise the aerospace and shipbuilding industries, increasing the concentration and centralisation of capital, and promoting the internationalisation of capital through collaborative weapons projects.

But the consequences of military spending for the sphere of production outreach the state's direct influence. They can best be traced by considering the question of productivity. It is often argued that military spending increases the growth of productivity through 'spin-off'. Arms production involves high technology requiring major investment in research and development. The argument about spin-off rests on two points: first, that only the state can finance this investment because of its scale; second, that the benefits of it are transferred to the civilian sector.

There are various examples of spin-off, ranging from biros through computers to nuclear power. The assembly line for mass production was first introduced for the manufacture of firearms in which the US machine-tool industry also had its origins in the late nineteenth century. Navies were among the first to use turbine engines in the years before the First World War, and new steel processes were developed first for use in armour plate and then used in other ways. In a 'near spin-off', a plan for the mass production of cars was presented to the board of Vickers, the great arms corporation, in 1906, two years before Henry Ford's Model T began production in the USA, but it was turned down. While the transistor and the integrated circuit were first developed with private civilian funding, their adoption by the military played an important role in promoting these two crucial innovations of the 1950s.[9]

However, the question of spin-off is more complex than first appears. What is important for productivity growth is *process technology* – developments which cut costs and increase efficiency in the way things are made. The major spin-offs before the First World War were to do with production processes. But military production now is most concerned with *product improvement* – the increasing capability, sophistication and complexity of successive weapons which was discussed in chapter 3 – and with this go rising real costs. The fact that there has been spin-off does not mean that it always occurs or is inherent to military spending. Nor does it prove that military spending was necessary in order to gain the new processes and technologies. A different allocation of resources could produce the same results over time.

There is also a different kind of effect, a negative spin-off from military spending. Since 1945 the arms companies and the military have developed an ever closer relationship. This has combined with the lack of competitive consumer-market pressures to make these companies inefficient. Their general record is of increasing costs and diminishing productivity growth. Military contracts sustain industrial capacity which is inefficient by civilian criteria and they support an extravagant technology of little relevance outside the specialised world of weapons.

In addition, dependence on military contracts by large companies appears to induce rigidities which inhibit adaptation and profitable growth. An early example was the Vickers' board's inability to see the potential in mass production of cars. A current example is the refusal of the management of Lucas Aerospace to push ahead with the projects developed by the shop stewards and presented in their Corporate Plan for the company in 1976. In US aerospace, it was companies like Lockheed and Grumman, which were the most dependent on military contracts, which ran into trouble in the 1970s and nearly went under, rather than companies like Boeing which makes bombers and air-launched cruise missiles but has also retained a strong orientation to the civil market for passenger aircraft. In corporate management, rigidities induced by military work often seem to seep into its civil work, influencing attitudes and performance there as well.

These problems have been recognised in the US electronics sector. Leading companies have been reluctant to tender for Pentagon contracts for very sophisticated microprocessors. This seems to result from concern that what the Pentagon wants is too sophisticated for the civil market, so the outcome would be reliance on further military contracts.

One executive claimed that taking military contracts 'means bureaucratic consensus and inertia in the selection of programmes instead of entrepreneurial insight and market driven exploration of new ideas.'[10] This in turn, it was thought, would lead to US companies losing out to Japanese and western European competition.

If spin-off were reliable and constant, such companies would be expected to recognise military work as a way of strengthening their civil operations. In fact, while they experience high productivity growth and increasing profitability in stable or expanding markets they are unlikely to want military contracts. They would seek them only when their growth and profitability are reduced by the rigours of competition, a collapse of the market or their own inefficiency. So it is likely to be the least profitable, efficient and flexible companies which seek military work. These are also the companies which would be least able to benefit from spin-off if the potential for it existed. If companies miscalculate and seek military contracts when they do not need to, the evidence suggests they will 'learn' rigidities which will seep into their civil work.

Corporate rigidity is one of the major ways in which military spending has the indirect effect of reducing productivity growth. We have already discussed the effect of military spending on investment, which also reduces productivity growth. Finally, the very availability of funds for military research and development, whether in corporations, universities or government research institutes attracts large numbers of scientists and technologists into military work. They and their skills are thus denied to the civil sector where, among many other things, their activities might contribute directly to productivity growth rather than waiting on the lottery of spin-off.

Unemployment

The relationship between military spending and employment is both controversial and politically sensitive. Trade unions seeking to defend members' jobs are often found defending military contracts, even though they may in principle support cuts in military spending. At a time of high unemployment, politicians find it easy to play on workers' justifiable fears of losing their jobs in order to undermine support for military cuts.

There are about 26 million people in uniform worldwide. In the absence of reliable figures, a rough estimate suggests that about 80 million people have jobs which depend on military spending, working in the military, in related government positions or in industry.[11] The controversy does not concern whether or not military spending provides these jobs, for it obviously does, but whether or not it is *necessary, effective* and *utilised* for job creation. Arguments on both sides of the controversy are to be found from both right-wing and left-wing theorists.

In exploring this issue, the first point is that the figures in Tables 4.1 and 4.2 reveal no systematic relationship between shares of output devoted to military spending and unemployment rates across countries. Nor does the econometric evidence suggest any systematic relationship over time.[12] Whether the comparison is national or international, the result is a random pattern.

This inconclusive empirical finding is supported by theoretical considerations. As discussed earlier in this chapter, increasing military spending at a time when aggregate supply exceeds aggregate demand would probably increase output and employment. The actual effect depends on numerous factors, and whether or not it is sustained over time depends on numerous other factors. But the reason why actual output is lower than its potential is more likely to be found in structural supply-side constraints rather than inadequate demand. In this more likely circumstance, the evidence is that the component of demand which makes the necessary adjustment is spending on investment. Over time, this translates into lower productivity growth and output than would otherwise have been the case. This in turn is likely to reduce the international competitiveness of the country's industries, leading to higher unemployment. But the precise role of military spending in losing jobs is as hard to calculate and as sensitive to as many factors as its role in creating them.

Much depends, then, on the circumstances in which military spending is increased. There is no fundamental theoretical reason to expect it to have one effect rather than another. Accordingly, arguments that military spending is necessary for job creation are entirely unproven. A different use of the same resources might create as many jobs. Similarly with arguments that it is effective in that role. Using resources differently might create more jobs. But, again, there is no general rule about the job creation effects of alternative uses of resources now devoted to military preparations. Everything depends on the specific alternative uses, on the circumstances in which the shift in allocation is made, on the particular problems of transition and how they are handled.

The third part of the controversy concerns whether states use military spending as a way of increasing unemployment. Despite arguments that jobs will be lost if military cuts are made, there is no clear evidence to support the proposition that job creation is a major goal of military spending. The current period ought to provide a useful test case for the hypothesis. But if the 1977 decision by NATO to increase military spending or the increases ordered in Britain and the USA in the early 1980s were made in order to increase employment, we can only say that they have been remarkably ineffective. In Thatcher's Britain and Reagan's America, raising military spending is not accompanied by a predisposition to use state intervention to create more jobs.

The connection between military spending and employment is indirect and swings on what we have already described about the role of US military spending in sustaining US hegemony which created stable conditions for capitalist accumulation until 1974. That period of boom and prosperity saw relatively low levels of unemployment. But the costs of its military role weakened the USA's ability to provide that stability, and one of the ways in which its passing is now registered is in mass unemployment.

Increased military spending in the early 1980s is part of a response to the international crisis, seeking to provide a political framework for economic recovery. If the crisis is resolved in the coming decade, it may again be possible to argue an indirect causal relationship between military spending and high employment, but only on the assumption, far from certain, that the resolution of the crisis actually does involve a return to higher employment levels. At the moment, it is easier to see how the ideology and coercive power of militarism could enable advanced capitalist states to survive the crisis than to see how military spending *per se* could generate a return to the low unemployment of the 1950s.

Economic motivations of military spending

The third of the problems we identified at the beginning of this chapter concerns whether and how far military spending is economically motivated. Before it can be addressed, the question of economic motivation needs some clarification, for a lot depends on the way in which it is asked.

A handy example is the USA's decision to purchase 3,400 air-launched cruise missiles from Boeing. One may ask about this decision, or others like it, whether or not the US government took it for economic reasons. It is more likely that the debates within the state emphasised strategic and military requirements. Boeing would certainly have tried to influence these debates since it wanted the contract for corporate economic reasons (i.e. profits). Whether this influence was enough to determine the decision is dubious. Pressure from the corporation was one among several pressures from bureaucratic, military and political sources. Its influence as a major component of the USA's military industrial infrastructure would be important, but not overriding. It would work with other factors to generate the impetus towards the decision to purchase the missiles.

Thus, for individual companies or the arms industry as a whole there is a clear economic motivation. But in this chapter we have been discussing the problem of overall military spending and the economy as a whole. Posed at this level, the question of economic determination is not the same as it is when posed at a corporate level.

Unfortunately, we also need to know whether we are talking about a direct economic determinism or a more indirect causation arising from the whole structure of capitalism. If the question is strictly economic, treating military spending more or less as an instrument of economic policy, our answer derives from our conclusions about the economic consequences of military spending.

In brief, if military spending is carried out as an instrument of economic policy it is either a very bad instrument or else the policy is very bad. Over time, military spending weakens the domestic economy. It leads to lower rates of investment, lower productivity growth and lower economic growth. Corporations which rely on military contracts tend to develop a structural ossification which seeps into the civil economy. It does not seem possible to argue that states spend on the military in order to achieve these effects. In that sense, military spending is not economically determined.

But there is another level at which the question must be posed. Military spending is necessary for the stability of capitalism and capitalist societies – necessary not because of the act of spending, but because of the power it provides both nationally and internationally and the ideologies associated with it. At different times, the particular function of military spending is different. At the onset of the first cold war, it aided the establishment of a new international system of economic regulation. With the new cold war, it represents an effort to shore up a system in crisis. The requirement for it is based on the long-term requirement for economic stability and growth, assessed and established in political terms.

Military spending is a complex and contradictory process. It erodes what it maintains; it buttresses what it undermines.

No simple functionalism or economic determinism can be adequate to explain it, either in general or in detail. Instead, to explain the economic phenomenon of military spending it is necessary to refer to the social, ideological and political fabric of advanced capitalism. Its complexities and contradictions derive from the complexities and contradictions of the social system which produces it and in which it functions.

5. The economics of disarmament

In Europe, North America and Japan there are now major mass movements seeking disarmament, especially nuclear disarmament. All of these movements make their arguments at a number of different levels. It is useful to put these various cases for disarmament into three categories.

First, there are arguments especially based on considerations of human survival. They point to the immense destruction which even a 'limited' nuclear war would cause. They point to the increasing emphasis in nuclear strategy, especially on the western side, on war-fighting and war-winning as opposed to pure deterrence. They point to the possibility in a crisis of a pre-emptive nuclear war, launched in the expectation that otherwise the other side will strike first.

Second, there are political and social cases for disarmament, in which we include essentially moral or ethical arguments. Variously, they point to the stultifying effect on national politics of entanglement in nuclear alliances and strategy, to the growth of militaristic attitudes, to the ethical erosion of societies prepared to defend themselves by the threat of 'omnicide'.

Third, there are economic arguments which refer to the distorted priorities evident in a world where millions suffer in poverty while resources are squandered in a futile search for security which only creates further insecurity. They point to the alternative uses to which these resources could be put in rich countries as well as in poor ones.

Combined, these arguments make a formidable case for disarmament, for progressively reducing arms and military spending, for seeking new arrangements for regulating affairs between states and new uses of the resources now devoted to military preparations. Opposing them are familiar arguments on the need for national security, the virtues of nuclear deterrence, the stability of a system of permanent confrontation. Underlying these arguments against disarmament there is a series of powerful preconceptions about the nature of international relations and the importance of national unity and social discipline. Caught between the mass disarmament movements and the defenders of current policy are those who share the establishment's preconceptions about the appropriate order of power in national and international affairs, but who share the disarmament movements' anxieties about the dangers of permanent nuclear confrontation and current strategies.

In previous chapters, we have insisted on the need to understand military spending as a complex and contradictory process, related to the basic requirements of nation states and international state regulation, reflecting the contradictions of the social system which produces it. From this insistence comes an obvious set of objections to disarmament, that whatever its apparent merits it would be economically and socially disruptive, internationally chaotic and politically impossible. To accept these objections is implicitly to accept the need to continue to squander resources and risk nuclear annihilation; but to ignore them is to demand political support and action for disarmament on the basis of a simple leap of faith into a utopian future. One of our aims in this concluding chapter is to point out an alternative between fatalism and utopianism.

It should be clear that part of the politics of disarmament must be a programme of economic demilitarisation. As military spending is reduced, the institutions, enterprise and activities which it now mobilises must be changed or replaced. There are two reasons for this and they handily summarise the aims of the economic component of a policy of disarmament, whether it is pursued by one state, a group of states or all states. First, without such a programme, permanent pressures for rearmament will remain. These pressures will be found both within the general fabric of state and society, and within the military, bureaucratic and industrial bodies which depend on military spending. One of the aims of the economics of disarmament will be to facilitate disarmament by disarming the opposition to it. Second, without such a programme, there can be no guarantee that the resources saved from military spending will be utilised in a more humane, sane and generous way. Yet that is one of the reasons for carrying out disarmament, one of the basic arguments for it. The economic policy within disarmament will have to encompass both functions.

The economics of disarmament are as political as the economics of militarism. That is, they concern basic questions of power in both international affairs and domestic society. Economic demilitarisation cannot be understood as a purely technical process, but there is within it a set of essentially technical problems. Understanding them and identifying solutions can both contribute to making the case for disarmament and develop practical policies to be available if the disarmament movements succeed in changing state policies. The discussion in this chapter begins with these issues, showing the role of technical solutions to the technical problems and indicating how they shade into the political questions at the core of the disarmament process. We start by considering this at a national level, then look at relevant issues in the international environment and conclude by returning to the political questions of militarism and disarmament.

Industrial and economic conversion

The task is to devise an economic policy which can facilitate the conversion of important parts of the arms industry to other uses. The more ambitious the disarmament programme envisaged, the more ambitious the task of conversion. At whatever level of disarmament ambitions the task is set, a whole range of interrelated issues will be faced, including: occupational conversion; re-use of industrial facilities; ensuring adequate demand for alternative products; changing the technological institutions; maintaining adequate aggregate demand; and the question of planning. In this section, we examine these issues.

Military industry generally employs a workforce which is more than usually skilled and specialised. One can regard the level of skill as an asset which will ease conversion, but the degree of specialisation as a problem. However, the problem of specialisation is often overstated. Studies have shown that most production occupations can convert directly to several kinds of non-military production. The work and the materials are essentially the same. In other cases, training for shop-floor workers would be required up to a maximum period of about six months. There is a comparable degree of occupational flexibility for most research and development staff, but studies have suggested that for some of these workers retraining periods of up to 18 months or two years could be necessary.[1] Thus, where occupational conversion encounters problems, the key to the solution is retraining, which would have to be matched carefully with the specific needs and requirements of the people involved.

This adaptability, surprising to many people as they encounter the relevant studies for the first time, is matched by the adaptability of much plant and industrial equipment. In certain cases, especially in electronics and also in aerospace if the demand existed, workers could be engaged in essentially the same tasks, in the same places, using the same equipment and materials. However, where re-equipment is required, as it will be in many cases, large investments will be needed. This could be kept as low as possible by a judicious choice of new production, and will not have to finance new factory buildings, office space or land purchases. It will nonetheless be a large-scale programme which will need careful planning and implementation.

All this will not make much sense if it results in producing things that nobody wants. The range of alternative products for converted military industry is very wide and includes machine tools, health equipment, education aids, transport, energy technology, construction, and more.[2] Capital goods could be produced for industry and government, and consumer goods for sale on the open market. Many of the alternatives are very exciting, opening new possibilities for more socially and ecologically responsible uses and development of technology. But to be taken up, these would require changes in government policy.

At one level, the problem of ensuring adequate demand for these products is a straightforward one – essentially, it requires proper market research. The problem is alleviated if central or local government form much of the market. It would be important to avoid initiating production in fields which meant immediate competition with well-established products and enterprises. Market penetration is a difficult and costly process; generating new markets is not easy either. But the experience of military industry in high precision work could provide a comparative advantage in some areas, as long as the tendency towards superfluous sophistication could be avoided. If trade were planned so that certain imports were restricted for a period, this could provide a breathing space for converted enterprises to establish their new production and markets.

At every turn here, however, the technical problems of conversion have begun to shade into political problems concerning government policy and attitudes to technology and trade. It is easy enough, on the basis of research studies carried out over a number of years, to identify alternative products and solutions to problems of occupational conversion and re-use of industrial facilities. But this whole process must be carried through in a receptive environment or it will collapse. This point is particularly important because of the pervading economic crisis which must form the context to discussing how to provide the right environment.

Technological institutions

The aspects of conversion we have discussed so far do not amount to a complete conversion of enterprises currently producing arms. Although skills and equipment can be transferred from one activity to another, it will be important not to transfer attitudes as well.

In military research and development, basic attitudes are structured around technological momentum. Progress is measured in product improvement and sophistication. The consequence of this is the expensive, over-elaborate and unreliable equipment which fills much of the most modern military arsenals. These attitudes which have become embodied in military management structures are quite inappropriate to the civil market, whether for government, industrial or individual consumption. Where this approach has been adopted for civilian products, e.g. Concorde, British Rail's Advanced Passenger Train, or the Advanced Gascooled Reactor, the results have been expensive failures. When these attitudes spin-off into companies' civil operations, the results have been poor.

Industrial conversion therefore necessitates institutional change. In general, a programme of conversion should minimise upheaval as much as possible. But in the case of research development and management, the rule is the more upheaval, the better. Design teams need to be broken up and dispersed. One way of achieving this would be through the retraining which would be required for some workers in research and development. The aim should be to gain the benefits of advanced technology without the ills. To do this, structures which maintain the current attitudes and approach of the arms industry will have to be demolished.

This is not a mere technical problem. It concerns at root the question of management prerogatives in industry. A government seeking to implement a conversion programme would have to take on the managements of the major arms corporations, gaining the support of the workers in the process. An important way of doing this would be to involve the workforce in the planning of conversion in each enterprise. It would have to guard against and have counter-measures for a flight of capital or a capitalists' strike. Once again, therefore, politics takes over from technical solutions in the economics of disarmament.

Aggregate demand

In the previous chapter, it was argued that the specific effects of raising military spending depend on various factors including the general economic environment and government policies on spending, taxes, finance and exchange. The same is true of reducing military spending.

The requirement is to gear the government's industrial and economic policies so as to maintain the level of aggregate demand and provide employment for those whose jobs formerly depended on military spending. In principle, this is a technical problem of no intrinsic difficulty. Various trials on econometric models indicate that appropriate mixes of tax cuts and increases in other government spending would minimise the transitional costs.[3] In the medium term, reducing military demand would feed back as higher investment and productivity growth. It is now fairly widely accepted that the economic problems of disarmament are short-term, technical and surmountable.[4] This optimism is reinforced by reference to the ease with which 8 million people in Britain were transferred from military to non-military work in the 18 months after the Second World War ended. The change was facilitated by the retention for a period of the wartime planning system. Even though it was also facilitated by a large exodus of women from paid work, which we would not want to repeat in a future disarmament programme, the experience does suggest that the smaller demobilisation now required is relatively straightforward. There is also the experience of the 1950s, when the Conservative government made a large reduction in military spending, without much planning of the transition, and without any increase in unemployment.

In practice, however, a transition to lower military spending in the 1980s would have to be accomplished in a very different environment. The context is not recovery from war as in the 1940s (though the problems of industrial reconstruction are similar), nor growth and relatively full employment like the 1950s, but mass unemployment and industrial stagnation. Economic demilitarisation will have to be accompanied by new policies to increase demand and sharply reduce unemployment. This means that an economic policy for disarmament will necessarily reflect overall social and economic objectives. The technicalities of the process will therefore reflect the politics which guide it. Whatever the political colouring of the programme, the key to it is to ensure adequate levels of demand. If this is not achieved, the programme will founder because it will impose severe costs on large numbers of people and lose political support.

The British case

Disarmament poses few economic problems as long as there is the political will, expanding demand, and industrial planning to co-ordinate conversion. The difficulty arises from ensuring that these preconditions are met. Nowhere are these difficulties more acute than in the UK. A century of relative decline, the international orientation of British capital, and restrictive government policies, have combined with world recession to produce an industrial wasteland. Thus Britain provides an instructive case to consider. It should be emphasised that the problems examined below are not peculiar to disarmament. They have to be faced in any case if Britain is to prosper. In fact disarmament could play a major role in creating that prosperity.

Over the past several years, left-wing groups and trade unions in Britain have discussed a series of proposals for economic recovery which have come to be known collectively as the Alternative Economic Strategy (AES). It exists in a confusing variety of forms and has generated a lot of controversy, some of which focuses on the specific problems of specific variants, and some on the inherent problems of reform programmes under capitalism.[5] We cannot enter into that controversy here. We share some of the general and specific misgivings about various versions of the AES, but we also believe that it could have the potential to improve the lot of many people and to democratise new areas of social relations. Ultimately, as with the prospects for disarmament, much depends on how the contending political forces stack up against each other and what tactical compromises can be effected without corrupting the basic intentions of the strategy. What we want to do here is briefly outline a general economic programme which draws on components of the AES, in order to indicate how disarmament could fit into it and strengthen it.

As well as disarmament, the policy involves five interlinked proposals. They constitute a package of mutually supporting elements which would affect production, exchange and distribution simultaneously.

First, *a general expansion in the level of demand* led by an increase in public spending would provide new employment, meet social needs and create the infrastructure for sustained growth through large-scale capital investment.

Second, *a general expansion in potential supply* would be based on restructuring industrial productive capacity through state intervention, including nationalisation and planning agreements.

Third, *the development of workplace democracy* would involve workers in the overall programme, match production more closely to needs, reduce the alienation of labour and probably improve productivity and the quality of production.

Fourth, *the planning of trade and movements of capital* would prevent increased demand from being met by increased imports (but need not mean a reduced volume of imports), provide industries with a breathing space for restructuring and developing new products, and constrain attempts by multinational companies to shift production abroad.

Fifth, *anti-inflation instruments*, especially controls on prices and profits supported by reductions in indirect taxes are needed to restrain inflation.

The question of import controls is a particularly sensitive one, and discussions of the AES often focus on it, to the exclusion of the other elements. There are three basic objections to import controls. First, it is argued that they would encourage inefficiency in the protected industries. It would be very important to ensure that the controls existed only long enough for new production to establish itself and that they did not amount to a ban on the import of any specific product or group of products. The second objection can be summarised as 'the export of unemployment'. Protecting industries in one country means restricting the market opportunities of industries in others where output and jobs would be lost. But most British proposals for import controls do not seek actual reduction in imports. Rather, they seek to permit higher levels of demand to be associated with lower levels of imports than would otherwise be the case. In a sense, imports can be controlled either by mass unemployment or by planning trade. There are numerous reasons why the second way is more desirable. The third objection concerns the risk of retaliatory import controls by other countries and a trade war. Protectionism, it is argued, breeds protectionism. Much here depends on the nature of the controls and on the international economic and political environment. At root, this objection concerns the international political resistance which a programme like the AES would generate, especially if it were associated with disarmament.

We thus come once again to the politics of economics. While it could not be the whole answer, an important factor in the political battle would be the extent to which domestic political support could be retained and even strengthened. This is why it is so important to include in any such programme, especially if it is associated with disarmament, a strong element of industrial democracy involving large numbers of ordinary workers in its development.

Economists of different schools would disagree about the extent to which state planning is required for economic demilitarisation. Many would argue that if the resources are 'released', they will find productive uses without state intervention. We think that if there is no planning, there is no guarantee that the resources will be utilised or, if they are, that they will be utilised in the best way. In the current crisis with the kind of industrial restructuring needed in Britain, there is an even greater need for state planning backed by legal provisions to enforce implementation.

Centralised authoritarian planning is notorious for the rigidities it introduces. This is a second argument for industrial democracy. However, this would need to be accompanied by the participation of representatives of the communities in which arms factories are situated. It is not only the direct workforce which has a stake in ensuring a smooth transition from one kind of work to another. Where feasible, potential consumers (e.g. area health authorities, transport committees) could also be involved to provide direct contact between those who will make and those who will use the new products. The involvement of the state will be required to ensure there is no duplication in new production and that local plans are feasible both technically and economically. This will entail a shift to new elements of democracy in the state itself.

Within the overall programme, cuts in military spending will have certain specific roles. Transferring it to the provision of urgently needed goods and services will give an immediate boost to consumption, and thus also strengthen political support for the programme. Military industry contains the resources in terms of skills and equipment which are needed to rebuild the productive base of the UK economy. It also absorbs a large proportion of research and development personnel. Reducing military spending would therefore also be a major way of expanding industry's innovative capabilities. With proper handling, disarmament measures could make a major contribution to demand, production and innovation.

However, innovation not only requires personnel of adequate levels of skill and training. It also needs a certain dynamism, a ferment of ideas and an institutional openness to those ideas. The experience of the shop stewards and their Corporate Plan at Lucas Aerospace not only showed the imagination and insight of development and production workers, it also revealed the institutional rigidity of the corporation in its initial blank and blind refusal of the proposals, and of the government in its inability to do anything positive. Democratic planning could open up the possibilities for taking on such ideas as those produced by the Lucas workers. This is a third argument for industrial democracy, and a further argument for sensitive economic planning.

We have emphasised that while the economics of disarmament involves a number of technical issues the politics will be paramount. This is true not only at the general level, the need to mobilise and organise around a coherent programme, but at the specific level of policies and institutions. The disarmament process will involve a lot of detailed choices and appropriate agencies will be needed both to plan conversion and to maintain momentum and coherence. The design of these agencies, whether they are ministries, quangos or commissions, is of considerable importance. Whatever the institutional form, the choices will have to be made in the context of some defence policy which provides an alternative framework for increasing UK security. The details of the construction of alternative frameworks and institutions is currently the subject of considerable work within the peace movement, and will be crucial to the politics of disarmament.[6]

The international environment

So far, we have discussed the problems of industrial conversion and economic recovery at a national level, assuming that Britain is the only country where disarmament measures are initiated. The disarmament movements, however, seek arms reductions in many countries either by agreement or through parallel unilateral actions. In general terms, both politically and economically, the more states that undertake disarmament, the better. With proper planning for industrial conversion in each country, and with the process directed at aiding economic recovery, the result would be that the expansion of supply and demand would be an international pattern and the world economy would become more buoyant as trade picked up and growth rates increased. Countries in which industrial conversion was not planned would probably do relatively less well with higher short-term costs in the transition and lower medium-term benefits.

In this kind of situation, the need for import controls in some countries might be less, but their imposition by others might be more of a problem. It would seem necessary to co-ordinate the planning of trade through an international agency, and to relate that planning specifically to the needs of the disarmament process and industrial capacity converted from military to civil uses. This would be a major task of international regulation, but if the conditions exist for international agreements on disarmament then they ought to exist for international agreements on trade.

That, however, is the fundamental question: could the right conditions exist for international disarmament agreements? The necessary conditions include a willingness to demote, if not banish, military power as a means of international state regulation. Such conditions presuppose major change in many countries, and the more ambitious the disarmament programme is, the more far-reaching that change must be. Whether or not it will be possible depends on the political will of masses of people.

Disarmament and development
The lavish military consumption of resources contrasts sharply with continued poverty in large parts of the world. There is consequently a growing acceptance of the need to transfer resources away from the military and into meeting the pressing needs of economic and social development in poor countries.[7]

At one level, the desirability of this transfer is undeniable, but the problems involved in it have rarely been examined in the necessary detail. Whether it were accomplished by means of aid or private investment projects, there are a number of pitfalls which must be avoided.

Aid can be a mixed blessing for poor countries. There does not seem to be a clear positive relationship between aid as a proportion of the recipient's gross domestic product and the rate of economic growth.[8] In fact, receiving aid can reduce the level and rate of savings which can cause serious long-term economic damage because aid is likely to be temporary and cannot substitute for sustained growth.[9] The transfer of resources ensuing from disarmament measures is likely to involve high technology. But the transfer of technology has also proven to be a mixed blessing. It is often associated with a bifurcated pattern of development in which a relatively skilled and prosperous urban proletariat and a new middle class exist alongside continued and even intensified rural deprivation and much poorer groups of urban workers and unemployed.[10] Politically, it is associated with new patterns of dependence. The control of technology is rarely transferred. This leads to continued reliance on the supplier countries and corporations. The latter increasingly site their production factories in poorer countries because labour is cheaper, while retaining development capacity in the advanced capitalist countries.[11] The enormous problems of social development in poor countries will be an obstacle to the proper utilisation of transferred technology. They are so great that even the best management of the process will not mean the benefits of disarmament will be enough to solve them.

These considerations suggest a number of guidelines. It seems particularly important in this context to eradicate the oversophistication of military industry when the technologies are turned to other uses. It also seems important to entertain relatively modest goals. The transfer of resources should be directed at meeting basic needs and constructing a basis for further economic development. This suggests strengthening international programmes against curable diseases, creating a strong infrastructure for essential services such as clean water and sanitation, education and health care, transport and energy, and undertaking medium-size agricultural and industrial projects. In all these efforts, the aim should be to transfer technological control as well as technology. For example, if machinery were used to improve agricultural output in a country, there should be a parallel project to develop the design and production capacity for that kind of machinery. Thus, as needs changed or as their specification altered, the country would not be relying on outside suppliers, having to persuade them to adapt their products to specific needs. Also this project should be related to programmes to strengthen the overall technical capacities of the country through higher education. In all of this, it does not seem that multinational corporations operating according to standard procedures are the best agents for the transfer of resources. Though it would not always be possible, it would be desirable to establish direct relations between those who are designing and those who will be using the products.

Working along these lines requires a political decision to do so on the part of all those involved in the process. If it were possible to achieve that, the potential contribution of disarmament to development in poor countries would be very considerable. The more states that are involved in disarmament, the greater the potential for development. But there will also need to be a major effort at international co-ordination, and this will doubtless become bound up in the contradictions within the poor countries and between them and the richer countries. Even in the best imaginable circumstances, disarmament will not neatly resolve those contradictions. The result will be to impede the smooth transfer of resources, and to make the benefits of it emerge more slowly. That should be expected. Easy solutions to these massive problems should not be envisaged. Properly handled, transferring resources from military uses in industrialised countries to civil uses in poor countries could help the latter a great deal. With some effort, the possibility exists for people in poor countries to benefit from modern technology without also becoming its victims. But basic problems of social, economic and political inequity cannot be simply wished away.

Disarmament in a militarist world

In this chapter we have time and again come to a point in the discussion where the adequacy of the economic instruments in a disarmament programme depends on political factors. Whether the issues of economic and industrial conversion are considered at a national or international level, the discussion can only go as far as showing how things could be managed if the political conditions were right. This is an important part of the argument. Favourable political opportunities for disarmament could be wasted if the economic component of the programme had not been thought through. A strong economic policy could build public support for further measures of disarmament as the benefits became clear. But part of our intention has been to show that demonstrating the economic possibilities and feasibility of disarmament is only a part of the argument.

Whether the first steps of disarmament are achieved by unilateral action or multilateral agreement, they must begin in a militarist and militarised world. They must start in a context of institutionalised permanent military confrontation and of a strong military component in international regulation of relations between capitalist states. The prevailing politics and ideology of the system oppose disarmament, however much politicians may say they want disarmament either to appease the peace movements or out of genuine conviction. Politics and ideology underwrite the economics of militarism and are strengthened by it. Our ambition must be to move to a situation in which politics and ideology underwrite the economics of disarmament and are strengthened by it.

It would be a contradiction in terms to rely for the first steps, or at any stage in disarmament, on the actions of those who manage and benefit from the international military order. They are part of the problem which the disarmament movements set out to solve. A political approach to disarmament which relies on their actions in diplomatic negotiations is simply turning aside from the main political impetus towards disarmament in the mass movements. This is perhaps the fundamental rationale for opting for unilateral measures of disarmament. The fabric of the military order will not come apart smoothly and simultaneously across all countries. Where splits in it appear, they have to be exploited. Of course, this approach must be supplemented by a range of social, political and economic arguments before it can be convincing; we summarised their main strands at the beginning of this chapter.

The problem which this raises is that if the political conditions for shifting state policy exist in only one country, the government attempting to implement disarmament measures will be internationally isolated. Other states will have an interest in penalising this government for stepping out of line. This is a particularly serious problem for a country like Britain which would be very vulnerable to economic retaliation. This is one reason why it is important that the disarmament movements be as internationalist as possible in philosophy and practice. Movements in other countries might be able to act so as to reduce the extent and the bite of retaliation. More importantly, the more countries in which state policies are shifted, the greater the chances that the change will be sustained. So although it is important to pursue unilateral initiatives rather than let disarmament languish in stagnant diplomacy, it is equally important to ensure that unilateralism does not become a form of isolationism or parochialism.

Some of the pressures against a disarming government might be mitigated by tactical modifications in both the disarmament programme and the accompanying economic policy. Opposition might be somewhat reduced by focusing initial disarmament actions on weapons systems which are particularly unpopular, expensive and useless, or by modifying control on trade and the movement of capital. Diplomatic moves might also help, attempting to make closer links with states which have an honourable record in seeking disarmament or, at a non-governmental level, invoking international trade union solidarity. In such manoeuvres, there is an obvious risk of so modifying the policy for tactical reasons that the initial thrust of it is lost. But in translating principle into practical policies, some compromise is almost inevitable, and the success of relatively limited first steps could help generate support for more ambitious further actions.

However, intelligent tactics are like a strong economic policy: they would help, but they are not the whole answer. In the end, this is a directly political question, a question of power, of how the contending forces stack up against each other. It concerns the degree of popular support for disarmament and the extent to which government policies can be geared to nourish that support. It concerns the extent to which what happens in one country is part of an international process of disarmament. It concerns the ability of disarmament movements to galvanise change and sustain it.

There is no way of guaranteeing that the political forces for disarmament will be stronger. We cannot even know the extent or the nature of the opposition to a disarming government, though we do know its sources. All that can be said is that if we are afraid of the opposition to disarmament, we might as well go home. That opposition is part of the problem we have set out to solve. In solving the problem, we shall have to confront opposition at all stages through a long process. It could not be otherwise.

Notes and references

Introduction

1. S. Aaronovitch and R. Smith, *The Political Economy of British Capitalism* (McGraw Hill, 1981). D. Smith, *The Defence of the Realm in the 1980s* (Croom Helm, London, 1980). E. P. Thompson and D. Smith (eds) *Protest and Survive* (Penguin, Harmondsworth, 1980). M. Kidron and D. Smith, *The War Atlas* (A Pluto Press Project, Pan, London, 1983).
2. These issues are discussed in more detail in R. Smith 'Aspects of militarism', *Capital and Class*, vol. 19, Spring 1983.
3. E. P. Thompson *et al., Exterminism and Cold War* (Verso, London, 1982) p. 1.
4. An introduction to some of these aspects is provided by P. G. Bennett and M. R. Dando, 'The arms race: is it just a mistake?', *New Scientist*, vol. 97, no. 1345, 17 February 1983.

1. Military expenditure

1. *World Armaments and Disarmament: SIPRI Yearbook* (Taylor & Francis, London); *The Military Balance* (International Institute of Strategic Studies, London); *World Military Expenditure and Arms Transfers* (US Government Printing Office, Washington, DC), all annual publications. Another similar compilation which is becoming increasingly widely used is R. L. Sivard, *World Military and Social Expenditures* (World Priorities, Leesburg, Va), also annual.
2. *SIPRI Yearbook 1980*, p. 15.
3. *The Military Balance 1980–81*, p. 13. Franklyn D. Holtzman, 'Soviet Military Spending: Assessing the Numbers Game', *International Security*, Spring 1982, pp. 78–101, provides a general critique of these estimates.

4. *SIPRI Yearbook, 1982.*
5. *Economic Report of The President 1980; British Economy Key Statistics 1900–1970*; B. H. Klein, *Germany's Economic Preparations for War* (Harvard University Press, 1959).
6. Evidence of M. E. Quinlan, in *Strategic Nuclear Weapons Policy*, Fourth Report from the Defence Committee, Session 1980–81 (HMSO, London, 1981) Minutes of Evidence, p. 111.
7. Cited in D. Wilkinson, *Deadly Quarrels* (University of California Press, 1980). Expenditure data come from G. Kohler, 'Determinants of the British Defence Burden', *Bulletin of Peace Proposals*, January 1980.
8. 'Falklands factor still imprecise despite £2.52bn estimate', *Financial Times*, 2 February 1983, p. 10.
9. N. R. Augustine, 'One plane, one tank, one ship: trend for the future?', *Defense Management Journal*, April 1975. Also see D. L. Kirkpatrick and P. G. Pugh 'Towards Starship Enterprise – Are the current trends in defence unit costs inexorable?' *Aerospace*, Journal of the Royal Aeronautical Society, 1983.
10. M. Kaldor, *The Baroque Arsenal* (André Deutsch, London, 1982).
11. R. P. Smith, 'Military expenditure and capitalism', *Cambridge Journal of Economics*, March 1977.
12. See S. Aaronovitch and R. P. Smith, *The Political Economy of British Capitalism*, chapters 6 and 7.
13. See *Business Week*, 18 February 1980.
14. R. P. Smith, 'The demand for military expenditure', *Economic Journal*, December 1980.

2. The drive to militarism

1. E. P. Thompson, 'Notes on exterminism, the last stage of civilization', in New Left Review (ed.), *Exterminism and Cold War* (Verso, London, 1982).
2. S. Aaronovitch and R. P. Smith, *The Political Economy of British Capitalism* (McGraw Hill, London, 1981) chapter 12.
3. D. Smith,, *The Defence of the Realm in the 1980s* (Croom Helm, London, 1980) chapter 4.
4. 'The decline of US power', *Business Week*, 12 March 1979.
5. See L. Thurow, 'How to wreck the economy', *The New York Review of Books*, 14 May 1981.
6. See D. Holloway, 'War, militarism and the Soviet state', in E. P. Thompson and D. Smith (eds) *Protest and Survive* (Penguin, Harmondsworth, 1980) pp. 151–54.

7. R. Bahro, *The Alternative in Eastern Europe* (NLB, London, 1978) p. 159.

8. D. R. Herspring and I. Volgyes, 'How reliable are eastern European armies?', *Survival*, September/October 1980.

3. The foundations of militarism

1. M. Kaldor, *The Baroque Arsenal*, (André Deutsch, London, 1981) chapter 2.

2. J. Downey, *Management in the Armed Forces* (McGraw Hill, London, 1977) p. 198.

3. Invaluable insights into how and why this occurs are provided by N. Dixon, *On The Psychology of Military Incompetence* (Futura, London, 1979).

4. See M. Knaack, *Encyclopaedia of US Air Force Aircraft and Missile Systems: Volume I, Post-World War II Fighters 1945–1973* (Office of Air Force History, Washington, DC, 1978); on the corruption in the buying and selling of the F-104, see D. Boulton, *The Lockheed Papers* (Jonathan Cape, London, 1978). J. Fallows, *National Defense* (Random House, New York, 1981) contains other examples.

5. See especially, 'Europe's F-16 plans unfold', *Flight International*, 23 October 1976; L. Kraar, 'General Dynamics struggles to build a plane for all nations', *Fortune*, March 1977; *Status of the F-16 Aircraft Program*, Report to the Congress by Comptroller General of the United States (General Accounting Office, Washington, DC, April 1977); 'War spurred lightweight fighter effort', *Aviation Week and Space Technology*, 2 May 1977; 'F-16: The multi-national multi-role aircraft', *Interavia*, January 1979.

6. As embodied for example, in F. C. Spinney, *Defense Facts of Life* (US Department of Defense Staff Paper, mimeo, December 1980).

7. M. Kaldor, *The Baroque Arsenal*, p. 185.

8. A. Krass and D. Smith, 'Nuclear strategy and technology', in M. Kaldor and D. Smith (eds) *Disarming Europe* (Merlin Press, London, 1982).

9. For example, G. T. Allison, *The Essence of Decision* (Little, Brown, Boston, 1971); M. Halperin, *Bureaucratic Politics and Foreign Policy* (Brookings Institution, Washington, DC, 1974).

10. N. Dixon, *On The Psychology of Military Incompetence*, p. 133.

11. M. Kaldor, *The Baroque Arsenal*, pp. 72–3.

12. C. Paine, 'Pershing II: the army's strategic weapon', *Bulletin of the Atomic Scientists*, October 1980.

13. On the Office of Systems Analysis, see A. C. Enthoven and K. W.

Smith, *How Much is Enough? Shaping the Defense Program 1961–1969* (Harper & Row, New York, 1971).

14. A. E. Fitzgerald, *The High Priests of Waste* (W. W. Norton, New York, 1972).
15. *Statement on the Defence Estimates 1982*, para. 407.
16. J. S. Gansler, *The Defense Industry* (MIT Press, Cambridge, Mass., 1980) pp. 39 and 185.
17 L. Kraar, 'Grumman still flies for navy, but it is selling the world', *Fortune*, February 1976.
18. J. S. Gansler, *The Defense Industry*, p. 129.
19. See E. A. Brown, 'Solution seeks a problem', *National Defense*, September/October 1976, one of a group of articles examining the military uses of lasers.
20. See D. Smith, *The Defence of the Realm in the 1980s*, (Croom Helm, London, 1980) pp. 95–102.
21. Useful examples of this are in J. Fallows, *National Defense*.
22. Arms trade data are tabulated each year in ACDA's *World Military Expenditures and Arms Transfers* and in *SIPRI Yearbook* (where they are also discussed); a summary of the data is in D. Smith, 'The arms trade and arms control', *RUSI & Brassey's Defence Yearbook 1982* (Brassey's, London, 1982). A theoretical discussion is provided in S. Sen and R. P. Smith, 'The economics of international arms transfers', Birkbeck Discussion Paper, 1983.
23. See A. Sampson, *The Arms Bazaar* (Hodder & Stoughton, London, 1977) and D. Boulton, *The Lockheed Papers* (Jonathan Cape, London, 1973).
24. SIPRI computer-stored data.
25. Unpublished research material, drawing on all publicly available sources.
26. *Ein Anti-Weissbuch* (Rowohlt, Hamburg, 1974) p. 83.
27. See *Two-Way Street* (Brassey's, London, 1979) and *Action Programme for the European Aeronautical Sector*, EEC Commission, Report to Council, 10 October 1975.

4. The economic consequences of military spending

1. *Business Week*, 4 February 1980.
2. R. P. Smith, 'Military Expenditure and Capitalism', *Cambridge Journal of Economics*, March 1977; and 'Military Expenditure and Investment in OECD Countries', *Journal of Comparative Economics*, March 1980.

3. *World Military Expenditures and Arms Transfers 1968–1977* (US Arms Control and Disarmament Agency, Washington, DC, 1979).
4. A. Maddison, 'Economic policy and performance in Europe, 1913–1970', in C. Cipolla (ed.) *Fontana Economic History of Europe: The Twentieth Century* (Collins, London, 1976).
5. *SIPRI Yearbook 1980*, pp. 66–68.
6. *Statement on the Defence Estimates 1981*, Cmnd 8212–II, tables 2.8 – 2.10.
7. Probably the best known exposition of this view is P. A. Baran and P. M. Sweezy, *Monopoly Capital* (Monthly Review Press, New York, 1966).
8. For a general review of underconsumptionism, see M. Bleaney, *Underconsumptionist Theories* (Lawrence & Wishart, London, 1976).
9. M. Kaldor, *The Baroque Arsenal* (André Deutsch, London, 1982) pp. 40, 41, 55 and 91; see also C. Trebilcock, 'Spin-off in British Economic History: Armaments and Industry 1760–1914', *Economic History Review*, December 1969.
10. *Business Week*, 27 November 1978.
11. M. Kidron and D. Smith, *The War Atlas* (Pan, London, 1983) map 27.
12. R. Smith, 'Military expenditure and capitalism: A reply', *Cambridge Journal of Economics*, September 1978; and G. Georgiou and R. Smith, 'Assessing the effect of military expenditure on OECD countries', *Arms Control*, summer 1983.

5. The economics of disarmament

1. These studies are discussed in, for example, D. Smith and R. Smith, *Military Expenditure, Resources and Development*, Birkbeck College Discussion Paper 87, November 1980; M. Kaldor, D. Smith and S. Vine (eds) *Democratic Socialism and the Cost of Defence* (Croom Helm, London, 1980); S. Melman (ed.) *The Defense Economy* (Praeger, New York, 1970).
2. See the works cited above; also the Lucas Aerospace Combine Shop Stewards Committee, *Corporate Plan* (mimeo, 1976); the Vickers National Combine Committee of Shop Stewards, *Building a Chieftain Tank and the Alternative Use of Resources* (Newcastle, 1978).
3. For example, V. Leontieff, *et al.* 'The economic impact – industrial and regional – of an arms cut', *Review of Economics and Statistics*, August 1965.

4. See, for example, G. Kennedy, *The Economics of Defence* (Macmillan, London, 1975).

5. For a debate on the AES, see *Socialist Economic Review 1981* (Merlin, London, 1981).

6. On institutions see B. Niven, 'An approach to defence industry conversion', (mimeo, SPRU, Sussex University, 1982); on framework see R. Bahro, 'A new approach for the peace movement in Germany', in E. P. Thompson *et al.*, *Exterminism and Cold War* (Verso, 1982), and the Alternative Defence Commission, *Defence without the Bomb* (Taylor & Francis, London, 1983).

7. See successive United Nations reports: *Economic and Social Consequences of the Arms Race and of Military Expenditures* (1972); *Reduction of the military budget of States permanent members of the Security Council by 10% and utilization of part of the funds thus saved to provide assistance to developing countries* (1975); *Economic and Social Consequences of the Arms Race* (1977).

8. D. Smith and R. Smith, *Military Expenditure, Resources and Development*, Birkbeck College Discussion Paper no. 87, November 1980.

9. T. Weiskopf, 'The impact of foreign capital inflow on domestic saving in underdeveloped countries', *Journal of International Economics*, 1972.

10. F. Stewart, *Technology and Underdevelopment* (Macmillan, London, 1977).

11. See D. Ernst (ed.) *The New International Division of Labour, Technology and Underdevelopment (Campus, Frankfurt, 1980)*.

Cynthia Enloe

Does Khaki Become You?
The militarisation of women's lives

More and more women are being drawn into an invisible khaki
net; not just as soldiers, but as a support system for the military,
who are dependent on women but do not like to admit it.

Cynthia Enloe looks at the many roles played by women in
relation to the military: as mothers and wives, as nurses,
prostitutes and social workers, as workers in munitions and other
industries dependent on military contracts.

She gives a feminist analysis of the army's use and abuse of
women, in Vietnam and in the Falklands, in the USA and in
Britain. She argues for urgent resistance to such military
manoeuvres.

'*Does Khaki Become You?* draws into a clear framework many
moving and enraging examples of exactly how far the military and
men in general can go in exploiting women . . . it makes inspiring
reading.' Connie Mansueto, Greenham Common activist.

'*Does Khaki Become You?* traces the military's ambivalence and
awkwardness in dealing with its dependence on women. Cynthia
Enloe's book is both informative and most absorbing.'
Nick Bloomfield, co-producer and co-director of the film *Soldier
Girls*.

272 pages   ISBN 0 86104 704 4   paperback   £4.95

Brian Easlea

Fathering the Unthinkable
Masculinity, scientists and the nuclear arms race

– Why does the arms race continue?

– Why do military-industrial-scientific complexes have such an
  insatiable demand for new weapons systems?

– Why does science co-operate so readily with this process?

In a lucid survey of science from Francis Bacon's 'truly masculine
science' to Robert Oppenheimer's devastating 'baby', Brian Easlea
shows how the seventeenth-century scientific revolution already
contained the seeds of today's oppressive technologies. He argues
for a revaluation of masculine institutions and ideologies, so that
science does not remain the willing accessory to man's war on
'feminine' values.

'Valuable contribution . . . buy it for any budding scientists you
know.' *Peace News*

240 pages   ISBN 0 86104 391 X   paperback   £5.95

These books are available through your local bookshop.
In case of difficulty write to: **Pluto Press**
                          Freepost (no stamp required)
                          105a Torriano Avenue
                          London NW5 1YP
To order, enclose a cheque/p.o. payable to Pluto Press to cover
price of book, plus 50p per book for postage and packing (£2.50
maximum). Requests for catalogues and other information should
be sent to the above address. Telephone 01-482 1973.